Twenty-Five Years Abroad

Larry B. Stell

ISBN 978-1-7361332-1-7 (paperback)
ISBN 978-1-956001-00-6 (eBook)

Copyright © 2021 by Larry B. Stell

All rights reserved. No part of this publication may be reproduced, distributed, or transmitted in any form or by any means, including photocopying, recording, or other electronic or mechanical methods without the prior written permission of the publisher.

Printed in the United States of America

FOREWORD

Larry B. Stell has written this book and dedicates his many abroad experiences to the many civilians, military and families, embassy and corporate families who live in other countries.

Overseas schools provide a unique opportunity for our elementary and secondary teachers to travel and see the world while working in their profession.

In this book Larry dwells deeply into his perceived concept of Americans abroad, in the international setting. His own perception of the European world was aptly acquired during his twenty plus years living abroad. The time span was 1960 to 1982.

In the 19 chapters of this book, he moves from his first assignment in Tripoli, Libya, where he taught biology for one semester, then, fortunately, he relocated to one of the best duty stations in Germany, Ramstein Air Base. He taught science in the Department of Defense Overseas Dependent School, Ramstein Junior High School, from January 1961 until June 1966. The rest his years abroad were spent in Italy, the Netherlands, and then Larry returned, again, to Karlsruhe, Germany, in 1971, which, at that time was the European Headquarters of the Overseas Dependent Schools.

The time spent abroad gave him the opportunity to witness the feelings and attitudes of Americans abroad, as well as those of Libyans, Germans, Italians, and the Dutch. His exposure enlightened him into a world perspective, and the limitations he would have suffered had he remained in the United States for his early adult years.

The richness he acquired through his second language, German, and living in four foreign countries enhanced his acquisition of self-awareness

The European experience is one he advocates for all young professionals in their early careers. He regrets he did not have an opportunity to live in the Orient, which he firmly believes would have broadened his perspective, in the world arena, even more!

CHAPTER 1

Desire to Live in Europe

I was brought up in Arkansas and was the offspring of a large family of nine. I enjoyed an exciting childhood, camped out, shot a BB gun, rode a horse, fished, hunted, and enjoyed life to the fullest. My mother and father owned grocery stores from the time I was born, in 1932, until we left Little Rock, Arkansas, in 1951, to return to the small southeastern town of Warren, Arkansas, where I lived from the age of three until I was nine years of age. My mother and father re-emerged after owning separate grocery stores. My father's store was in Tinsman and my mother's was in Warren. The separation came about because of strong desires of my mother and father wanted to expand their entrepreneurship and increase their capital.

When I attended the University of Arkansas at Monticello, Arkansas, 1951-1957, with a two-year intermission to serve in active reserve with the United States Navy from 1952-1953, I began to acquire my appetite for Europe. After resuming my studies from 1952 to 1957 I acquired a strong urge to either live in France or Germany.

The overwhelming tales of occupied Germany by discharged occupation troops returning to Warren, Arkansas, and various places in southeast Arkansas, whetted my desire to eventually go abroad and enjoy the visions I had conceived from these troops. The various foods, enchanting snow scenes, and warm guesthouses (Gasthäuser) of especially Germany created an almost haunting curiosity about this country. As I studied European History at the University of Arkansas, then Arkansas A & M, the beautiful descriptions of architecture, art, rulers, the Holy Roman Empire, and many wars, only accentuated my longing for Europe.

My experience in the United States Navy began to enhance my toleration of varied ethnic groups-African Americans, Polish, German, and other origins milling around my barracks in cold Great Lakes Training Center in February-April in 1952. The tales of various European foods, dances, and cultural contrasts to my own, only compounded this strong never ending desire to "get the hell out of Dodge," and see something even more exciting than just Milwaukee or Chicago. Then later duty assignments such as Norman, Oklahoma, San Diego, only added to the curiosity of "What would it really be like, to see and experience Europe?" The San Diego duty station allowed me to visit Hollywood and other cities around Los Angeles.

Even weekend liberty around Hollywood, with the moguls driving Mercedes, Jaguars, or foreign Italian automobiles, perpetuated my insatiable desire to depart these United States, pounce upon Europe, and swim in its dynamic culture.

I had chosen teaching as a career and completed my master's degree (sociology/social studies), in 1959 at Vanderbilt Peabody University in Nashville, Tennessee and had a couple of years teaching experience. I then began to dwell upon the idea of eventually working with the Overseas Dependent Schools, under the Department of Defense. I was grateful to have a profession that provided me with the opportunity to live almost anywhere in the world.

My two years at Vanderbilt Peabody University, in Nashville, Tennessee, and my rich experience of teaching at Ridgewood Preparatory School in Metairie, Lousiana, on the outskirts of New Orleans, intensified, even more, my desire for the restaurants and wines of Europe. Also, the better restaurants of Los Angeles and San Francisco, while bouncing around California, only added to my strong, insatiable desire to make the swift transition to the continent of Europe.

It was in Nashville, Tennessee, where I met, not only many foreign students, but some very elite families who spent summers abroad, either in Europe or Mexico. Continual discussion with people who spent time out of the United States on visits continued to whet my strong desire to expose myself to other cultures and see distant lands. Some of the foreign students were South American, Indian, Italian, German, French, Greek, or African, to name a few.

I recall having a Philosophy of Education, French Canadian professor, Dr. Hall, who readily and freely, spoke the French. I admired, envied, and respected his command of a second language. It would be later in life that I would acquire a command of German, learn some Italian, and even a little Dutch, because of the countries I would some day live in.

As the 3 quarters of graduate school were extended from the summer of 1958, then a year of teaching in a great private school in Metairie, Louisiana, through the summer and fall of 1959. I enhanced my studies by chasing beautiful women on the campus of Vanderbilt and George Peabody College for Teachers in beautiful Nashville, Tennessee. With some interesting courses in education philosophy, statistics, and cultural anthropology, I dwelled in my books, enjoyed the tastes of the local women, listening to jazz in Printer's Alley. I also philosophized with many music students who were lost and frustrated, particularly with their studies of music theory. This seemed to be the course that overwhelmed many of my music major friends at George Peabody College for Teachers, as it was then named.

I never ceased to be fascinated by some of the music majors because of their love of the arts. George Peabody College for Teachers, at that time, and I presume even now, had a great name for its school of music. Some told me on the campus, that it was even comparable to The Julliard School of Music in New York, though I never really checked out the validity of this statement. The summer musical concerts and various programs on campus of Peabody College, as it was often called, were excellent. It would be years down the road that I would be able to enjoy operas in various parts of Germany.

The constraints of graduate school studies, at the age of 26 years, and the lack of money, certainly prevented me from wandering outside of Tennessee. With the exception of a trip to Florida, with one of my friends studying geography and music, I spent my leisure time around Nashville. Most of my time was spent listening to concerts or lectures of such greats as Werner von Braun, the famous rocket scientist, or visiting various clubs that hosted good jazz artists.

My teaching experience in 1958-59 led me to New Orleans, a city, in my opinion, that whetted my appetite for wines, fine liqueurs, great food, and charming nightlife. I suppose I should also mention some of the exciting and voluptuous women whom I escorted about New Orleans. I believe it was on Canal Street and in the Roosevelt Hotel, where I often listened to a great pianist, Joe Burton, if I recall the name correctly. I would often take a date to hear him, or perhaps go by Pat O'Brien's for some of the dueling pianists playing fight songs and stimulating the tourists from various parts of the nation.

New Orleans was the one city I lived in, contrasted to Los Angeles or San Diego (my U. S. Navy assignment) that had such an appeal that I always felt as a true and warm home. I would make trips back to my home in Warren, Arkansas, to visit my family, but when I reentered fantastic New Orleans, I knew I was returning to my home, although a resident there for only one school year.

My acquaintance with Mr. O. O. Stuckey, owner of Ridgewood Preparatory School in Metairie, one of the suburbs of New Orleans, gave me a warm and welcome feeling in New Orleans. I profited, not only because of the contacts offered by him, since he had some of the solid backbone of New Orleans society and local business world attending his school, but also because of the charm of the Jewish, Protestant, and Catholic families who contributed to the school's structure and aurora.

I remember event in Ridgewood Preparatory School and it was the case of one of the students, a junior or senior, who was caught cheating on an exam. The student's mother owned one of the exclusive and famous restaurants in the French Quarter, and was removed from the school. The daughter had run out of private schools because of similar egregious acts in her prior schools. It seems that our director, Mr. Stuckey, had the privilege of removing the students, because of a well-drawn up contract, and did not have to refund tuition in such cases, or so I heard from his assistant, the headmaster of the school.

The association with the students of Ridgewood alone made the New Orleans experience worthwhile. I would almost wager that there wasn't one of the students in our school who had seen as little of the world as I had at the time. All of them were from well off families and most had traveled extensively.

On a recent trip to New Orleans, and while waiting for a return flight to San Diego, where I spent my recent years of 1985-2001, I called one of my previous students. He is a young man named Michael, whose family was the owner of a large jewelry store now located, in Metairie, where his parents lived and where Ridgewood was located. He told me that a few years ago, the family relocated the store to Metairie because activities in the suburbs offered better business opportunities, according to Michael. Michael made me promise to call him on any future returns to New Orleans so he could invite me to dinner. I failed to keep that promise, Michael, and I must apologize. But if this book is published, then maybe I shall do so. Reasons being that I shall then be able to return more often to New Orleans, a city I so well love, and then invite you to dinner.

I would visit New Orleans in the 1970s, on returns from Europe, then go by the well-known jewelry store and chat with the other son Larry Berger. I also remember a daughter of that family because three of them would ride the bus I drove each day to Ridgewood and pick up about 20 students. Driving the bus was a supplement to the salary I earned in the late 1950s and also gave me a chance to learn the streets of New Orleans, making the city even more familiar and warm.

I lived in a fantastic apartment on St. Charles Avenue, not far from the Lake Ponchartrain Hotel, and savored the romantic atmosphere of the Garden District of New Orleans. It was in an old Victorian house that had been made into apartments. It had high ceilings and was furnished with usable furniture, good enough for my one school year longevity from 1958 to 1959.

It was only recently that I read a book written by William Faulkner, called Pylon and it dwelled on some racing pilots back in the 1930s, and focused on New Orleans setting. I read the book with fond memories, as Faulkner depicted some of the intricate visions depicting many streets of the "Big Easy." It seems that the charms existing in the 1930s, remain today, especially as one wanders around the French Quarter and the Garden District of this charming city.

My experiences in New Orleans are a passionate indentation in my memory bank and I often return to the city, trying to grasp the fond memories I had while living there. It was in Pat O'Brien's in the 1970s when I returned with my wife and daughter, and made a comment to a bartender in the booming tourist site, asking, "Do you remember a certain Tulane U. v. Alabama U., perhaps a bowl game of 1959?"

His reply: "How in the hell should I remember something that happened here that long ago?"

End of friendly discussion with that bartender.

But now I go back there, enjoy the food, riding the St. Charles Avenue streetcar, trying to locate my old apartment on St. Charles Avenue, trying to envision the most pleasant experiences of bringing charming women to my enchanting apartment, or just reminiscing.

After the year in New Orleans, I left, with the headmaster of Ridgewood almost begging me to stay and teach the next year. But with the disillusionment of teaching, especially in the junior high part of the school, I was well beaten down, especially from the age level of the school I taught-grades 7-9. Even though it was a great school, the director tended to overload classes. It was mostly from a money/profit motive. Some of the classes with "super" spoiled brats, many having wealthy parents, that created a desire to rest or take a break. I was also overwhelmed by a need of self-d improvement and to pursue my master's degree. Vanderbilt Peabody University seemed to be the ideal place to dwell into studies.

O.O. Stuckey, the owner/director of Ridgewood, was grooming me for better things. At the time I could not see it but since I joined his church, the Baptist Church on St. Charles Avenue, he was monitoring my progress and grooming me as a second year teacher, at his school. But he obviously did not know my inner feelings regarding the strains of dealing with the larger numbers in the classrooms. I think, that if he had, he would have gone to no ends in trying to make my situation more comfortable. The reason I know he did like my profile is that in the early 1970s, he wrote me a letter when I was teaching in the Netherlands, with the AFCENT (Allied Forces Central Europe) Dependent Schools, and ask me if I would like to take over the school.

I presume that O.O. Stuckey also calculated that I had saved a great sum of money and would be able to handle the financing. I was young enough that I could possibly have taken over the school, with adequate financial backing, which I believe he would have directed me to. But he died not long after and must have seen the handwriting on the wall with the tremendous stress he received in running the school from its inception, until it blossomed into one of the better private schools around New Orleans.

After completing graduate school, it was off to Glendale, California to live with my brother, Dave, who was working for our oldest brother in the lumber business. After a few tears shed from Toni, one of my gorgeous young graduated student at Vanderbilt Peabody University, I was on my way to California with Dennis McCrary, a friend whom I acquired during the summer quarter of 1959. Dennis wanted to stay with me in California for a couple of weeks, which he did, then catch a ride back with some of his friends. Dennis had not completed his undergraduate degree so had a couple of semesters remaining in order to acquire his bachelor's degree.

The ride to California was exciting, using the old Route 66 to trek to California in my 1959 Chevy Impala, 2-door hardtop. We eagerly arrived at my brother's house on Buckingham Rd., a very nice part of Glendale, California. My oldest brother had bought the house and only lived there a couple of years while working as a sales representative for a large lumber company located in Louisville, Kentucky.

After the two weeks, Dennis returned to Nashville to resume the spring quarter of school. I submitted substitute applications for the city of Glendale, where I spent the spring teaching secondary schools. Before the spring semester of 1960 was completed, I had offers of almost any school of my choice to teach in the fall of 1960. Since I had just acquired my master's degree, I was, at my age of 28, quite sought after as a young teacher with adequate qualifications in social studies and physical science.

After enjoying the vicinity of Southern California, the Glendale area being close to San Diego so I could visit my mother and another brother,

James C. Stell, then an engineer with General Dynamics Corporation, I felt I was again back with my family. It was very fortunate for me since my future was to take me on a journey to Africa and then Europe, which would be a career in education for the next 25 years!

Southern California, especially the Glendale area, had that smoggy aroma at about mid-day. The sun bursting out about midmorning, in all its glory, the smog laws had not come into full blossom, and one's eyes could easily start burning on warmer spring days.

There were many days of breakfast in Bob's Big Boy, or other fast food restaurants or enjoying a nice breakfast with my brother David most of the time. David and I enjoyed the rather large home of my oldest brother and Dave rented out part of it to a family who had just spent five years working in France, with both children, one 13, and the other 19 and in junior college in Pasadena. The whole family was quite continental and pursued contacts of many French and European people in the area. The whole family learned French while tour with Radio Free Europe, I believe, and their continental ways impressed me. I loved hearing them converse in French, especially when they wanted to say something we should not hear.

But the whole purpose of speaking French was they wanted to keep up their practice of utilizing the beautiful language. It seems that both the children had attended French schools so were fluent in French. I was impressed and it just created a stronger desire in me to travel abroad and eventually find my target countries of Germany, France, or Italy.

This was just another piece to the puzzle, nudging me to pursue a career overseas. I remember one party with about 60 guests coming over to utilize my brother's house and the Fox daughter, who attended Pasadena Community College, had left it in disarray. My brother Dave contacted the dean of the Pasadena Community College since most of the party participants were from that institution. He submitted a complaint about the house being somewhat battered after the party. The family living there took immediate action and many of the party participants returned after the complaint and cleaned the house perfectly!

At any rate, I continued to socialize with the family and found them perfectly charming, other than the fact they were not the best housekeepers. We all shared the kitchen, but somehow, seemed to work it out with our somewhat commune state of existence. Actually my brother and I shared an end bedroom and a closed veranda, with our own private bath. Since my oldest brother, Max, owned the house, he granted my brother Dave the final say as caretaker. The family was quite congenial in their agreement with my oldest brother about rent money and general care.

I was, of course living in my brother's house, rent free, and only had to support myself by buying some food now and then. Since my brother Dave and I enjoyed doing thing together we could make weekend trips to Las Vegas, San Francisco, and other areas of California and enjoy the very nice area, almost in tourist fashion, always having the nice home to return to. We both had cars so were free to come and go as we pleased. My oldest brother, Max, employed David and he made various trips around California and Nevada selling lumber or lumber related merchandise. He had a nice new model Ford Station Wagon that was leased through my oldest brother's business so we traveled about the State of California and Nevada in comfort.

I dated many lovely women in the area, and even took out one of my senior students I had in class while substituting but only after she graduated. She was very attractive and graduated from Glendale High School in June of 1960. We dated up until I left for Africa, once she graduated from high school.

I was twenty-eight years of age and had the appearance of a nineteen year old, with the pleasant experience of having my I.D. often checked in night clubs around Glendale and Hollywood. I could "rob the cradle," so to speak, and still pass for a teen. It was a lovely situation.

It was the spring of 1960 and I began interviewing, seriously, for positions that would get me out of the field of education, because I could see the teaching rut creeping upon me already. If I were to remain in the United States, teach secondary school, and really become bored, then what a dull life I would lead! Or would I look for a corporate position, and I had decent qualifications, at least in the "education qualified," arena. I was young enough to be valuable to some firm or corporation, had a master's degree, and had taught a couple of years.

I was interviewed by an executive from Sears who wanted to hire me in an executive trainee position, and was almost livid when I did not jump at the offer. Another representative of Ford Motor Corporation offered me a position as a corporate representative to go to Japan. That is one I almost accepted, but at the time, I had a stronger desire to go to Europe, so I refused that position, knowing there was still a possibility I would click in my aim at Europe.

There were several more interviews, but all seemed to involve positions that would in some form or fashion, lead me down the road to boredom! I wanted to go to Europe, or in that direction because I absolutely, without a doubt, wanted to fly east after I acquired the right position.

It was in my substituting experience that I began to meet some teachers who had been with the Overseas Dependent Schools, some had been to Japan; others had been to Europe. There was one gentleman especially, whom I met and he had worked for two years in Germany, with his wife. He was with the U. S. Army Dependent Schools, and they allowed married teachers to do two-year tours abroad. It was the Air Force Dependent Schools in the 1960s that were restricted to only single teachers, female or male. Later, such restrictions were lifted.

These teachers keenly stimulated my desire and curiosity to no end. I got excited just talking to teachers who had spent time abroad with the Overseas Dependent Schools. I got more interested and inquisitive, then asked how one went about such a venture, especially since I was single, had a master's degree, and was extremely interested in going abroad to teach.

I was told that the U. S. Post Office had such information and there was a recruiting station in downtown Los Angeles at the time, and I should turn in such an application to the Department of Defense Dependent Schools. I wasted no time in making a trip to my local post office in Glendale, then filled out the application and anticipated some sort of reply regarding my inquiry.

After a few weeks I received the reply and was told to report to the recruiting center in downtown Los Angeles. My brother, Dave, always an opportunist, thought he would tag along, and also seek employment overseas. We were both single, adventurous young men who wanted to expedite our desires to climb the mountain of adventure and excitement on this earth, so we took the trip to the recruiting office.

Dave and I both were always seeking better positions than the existing ones we had, and I remember one position, a corporate one, we applied for. I came out better on the mathematics part of one of the tests, which qualified me for a position and I got the offer but it was another one I turned down, so it didn't matter anyway. The only thing I had in mind was getting to a foreign country, of my choice, then delving in other cultures and languages.

It was a spring day that Dave and I made our way into the recruiting center but one of us ended up being disappointed. We were to learn about the requirements of the Overseas Teaching program with the military, and there were various restrictions. Fortunately, at this time, one did not have to apply before January 1 of the year one was to teach in, as I now understand exists for the Overseas Dependent School System. If one has any ideas about pursuing the overseas school programs, especially with the Department of Defense, one must make sure the application meets their deadlines. An applicant will not be picked up at just any time and the person applying must submit the paperwork before January, even to be considered the year after.

At any rate, after interviewing at the recruiting center, we found out that if one had not been teaching a full year, but working in another field, such as business, then one was not qualified. My brother Dave, a previous teacher, had been working for my oldest brother, Max Stell, and had been out of teaching for about a year and a half. We both got up from our chairs disappointed, after talking to the recruiter.

"Gee," I replied, "I really wanted to get into this program! I am one disappointed person, because I have spent this last year substitute teaching, but only this spring semester. My summer and fall were spent in graduate school completing my master's degree, what a disappointment! I taught with a contract down in New Orleans prior to that."

"Wait a minute," replied the recruiter, "Did you say you had been working on, and completed your master's degree, but taught previously to that?"

"Yes, that is what I said."

"Oh, he replied, then you are eligible!"

"Am I really?" I replied questioning.

"Really! You are eligible for our program overseas. Go ahead and complete the application forms, please." The recruiter responded.

My brother, angry, and disappointed that he did not meet the requirements, grabbed my shoulder and then told me, "Let's get the hell out of here!"

"Wait a minute, I replied, you heard the man, I have the requirements."
"But you aren't interested, are you?"

"You bet I am interested," I replied.

It was then that I turned around, the gentleman gave me the form to fill out and I took it from him. It was to be sent back to Virginia, or that vicinity, and I gladly took the form. We said our farewells, then returned to my brother's beautiful home in the lovely hills, not far from downtown Glendale.

I filled out the required paperwork, stating that I had my master's degree, and had been completing my coursework the past fall. My degree was conferred in the spring of that year, 1960. I also marked the box saying that I would go any place in the world, hoping that stating I would go any place might put me in Europe or near Europe. It was at this point that I did not realize that the Overseas Dependent Schools always suffered from a lack of personnel who did not want to go to some out of the way places in the world.

When I did finally receive a reply from the recruitment office back east, they said I had been selected for a teaching position in Iceland.

"Iceland!" I shouted to my brother, "Hell, I do not want to got to Iceland, and will not go to Iceland! It is cold as hell up there, and even though I love to hunt, I am not going to that area!"

"I could have warned you about what you would be selected for, laughed my brother."

"Bullshit," I replied. "No way am I going to Iceland!"

I wrote back my reply, rejecting the offer. I thought this would be the end of the opportunity, and I would have to wait until the next year. But I got a call from the Alexandria, Virginia and one of the recruiting personnel made a comment to me via telephone.

"You signed that you would go anywhere in the world with our program."

"Well that may be true, but I am not going to Iceland. It is too far out of the way, and too cold up there, so I will not take the assignment."

"Alright, he replied, you will hear from us in a few days, and we can possibly give you an opportunity for another location."

"Fine, because Iceland is just not the place for me, so I would certainly appreciate something with milder weather and in the European vicinity," I politely replied, then hung up the phone.

In about 10 days, in early July after school was out and my substitute jobs were completed, I got a reply from the recruitment office. They stated that I had been selected to take a high school position teaching general science or biology in Tripoli, Libya, along the coast of North Africa. This one, I would also have to think about. I was to call back and accept verbally before I was to receive the paperwork.

After some arguments about whether there were lions in North Africa, or not, and viewing it on the map, I decided, because of its location, not far from Southern Europe, it would not be too bad.

Art Dalzel, a friend of mine I had met at USC, and a miler who ran with Wes Santee, and graduated from the University of Kansas, argued there were no lions presently in Libya. I did some research and found that he was right.

"You know what, Dave, I think I will take that assignment in Libya!"

"Are you crazy? You will not like that country. It is too far from everything, and I think it is worse than Iceland."

"Too bad," I replied, "I am going to take the assignment, even though I will remain in the teaching field. Teaching abroad is not the same boring rut one gets into teaching stateside!"

After much pleading and coaxing, my brother failed to influence me, even a little bit. I was going to Libya! With its proximity of Southern Europe and Egypt, a place I had always dreamed about, especially after being inspired by Jo Stafford's lovely song, "You Belong to Me," I was convinced that "the pyramids along the Nile" would be a great place to visit while living in Libya. The words of this song stimulate me even to day:

"See the pyramids along the Nile, See the jungle when it's wet with rain," I am still turned on by this song and want to jump into a plane and fly somewhere exciting every time I hear the recording.

The arguments from my brother were not convincing enough. My friends, quite a few, whom I had met while substituting in the Glendale area, were almost as excited as I was when I told them about my future plans.

"Wow, you are going abroad, and to North Africa!"

"What a lucky person!"

"You do like adventure, don't you?"

Such comments instilled further inspiration to take on the adventure, I now could not be stopped. I was even more exciting to my various dates, young ladies in their twenties, because I was about to expand my horizons and escape the monotony of living and teaching or working in the United States. I wanted more-I wanted something that would enhance my psychic, challenge my existence, and expose me to cultures quite different from my own.

It was in mid July, I believe, that I received a "port call," the date and location of my departure. I received military orders that allowed me to receive a commercial ticket to Charleston, South Carolina, where I was to depart, around August 22, 1960, for Tripoli, Libya.

I called all my close friends and told them about my future adventure. My mother took my car because she was visiting my brother in San Diego. Everyone in my family was quite excited about my future abroad. I had learned in the U. S. Navy, one can always return home!

CHAPTER 2

Impressions of Libya

After boarding Delta Airlines at LAX, and heading for Charleston, South Carolina, in late August 1960, knowing that the packers had picked up my two footlockers that contained my sole belongings, I was on my way. The strength of an elephant could not have pulled me back and make me reject this offer with the Overseas Dependent Schools.

After arriving in Charleston, and an interesting evening enjoying my dinner at a lovely seafood restaurant, I began to meet some more teachers who were to be on my flight to Libya.

As I reflect back on my preparations for the venture to Libya, I realize that the recruitment office of the Overseas Dependent Schools, had given me fair notice that one should have about $800 to $1,000 saved up before departure. This was to get one through the expenses before receiving a paycheck from the federal government. This did not really bother me since at that point in my life, I never seemed to worry about money, and always seemed to have enough in my hometown bank. Having money at this time of my life is something I still cannot figure out, unless it was that I was much more frugal then than now.

Reflecting back, I am sure that living and working abroad whetted my appetite for travel and fine restaurants, so today I enjoy the finer things of life, even though I cannot always afford the things I desire most. The many years abroad exposed me to other languages, the opera, other cultures, and a taste for multi-ethnic foods.

My orders directed me to the U. S. Air Force Air Base in Charleston, and I and about 63 other teachers found a Constellation, the 4-engine plane then used by the U. S. MATS (Military Air Transport Service), waiting for departure. We departed the next evening, after I arrived in Charleston, South Carolina at about 3:00 p.m., if I remember correctly. The date was about March 25, 1960.

I checked into a reasonable priced hotel and spent the day looking around Charleston, a lovely southern city I had never before visited. It would be years after, in the 1970s when I would return to Charleston from Germany.

I met some lovely ladies who had been teaching years for the system, had been to Japan, Philippines, Okinawa, Korea, and other foreign countries about the world. Our conversation was friendly and congenial.

I met one lady, blonde, quite attractive, in her forties, somewhat old for me, a lad of 28 years, and was ready to take care of me from that day on. Later I backed away from the relationship, but remained her friend as long as I can remember.

We departed from the U. S. Air Base in Charleston in the late afternoon the next day, August 26. Our plane was full of teachers, both elementary and secondary, along with several administrators. There were also some military families aboard but on this plane there were about 80 % educators. It seemed that everyone, with eyes on an overseas location, were seemingly on equal footing. There did not seem to be any class distinction between teacher and administrator, not like the typical school setting in the stateside environment.

Our plane stopped in Bermuda, dark and balmy, then trudged on to the Azores for an early morning stop. I remember the base on the island where we stopped was rather misty, windy, and it was early in the morning. I had already heard exciting voices rattling on about our ability to use base facilities, P.X., Commissary, and Class VI store (the military name for a liquor store). We were now full-fledged employees of the U. S. Department of Defense, and were entitled to all the goodies! This, in itself, was exciting. I knew that my cost of living from here on would be reduced considerably. I think one can expect the reductions compared to civilians living at home to be by about 30%. To this day, the advantages I had do not bother me and I feel that the military or those working for the military are certainly entitled to the bonus!

The plane droned on toward the coast of Africa and I continued to meet many of my future elementary and secondary comrades who would be working with me at Wheelus Air Force Base, Tripoli, Libya. About 50 or more educators were on that plane and most of them were either first year teachers for Wheelus Air Base. Also, most of this group was first year teachers in the program. I would suspect there were only about 25% being transferred from the Orient because to make the move to Europe, the teachers usually had to do a year in a less desirable area such as Libya, Turkey, or Ethiopia in order to get to the Continent of Europe.

I reflect back to an elderly lady sitting next to me on the Delta Airlines flight from Los Angeles to Charleston, South Carolina. She suggested that I take notes about my first impressions when I landed in Libya. I did this, and wrote an article for my hometown newspaper, and it was published in the fall of 1961 or early 1961. I have returned to Warren, Arkansas, and am trying, to this date, to find the article in their archives, but to no avail. I shall continue my search since the article covered not only a part of the first page, but also a large part of a second page of the Warren, Arkansas Eagle Democrat. I want to read it to review my impressions as a young man of twenty-eight years of age and my reaction to a strange country, so far away from home.

To say the least, the impressions of a completely new culture were quite spectacular, from my memory, to a twenty-eight year old person encountering a new language, and by all means a new geographical location in which I would be living for the next year. The Moslem activities, with workers about the base praying to Allah each day, were most impressive to a lad from Arkansas. The interaction with the Moslem world and trying to get a grasp on the language, 100+ degree Fahrenheit temperatures, and contrasting habits of Arabic people certainly blew my mind, to say the least.

I remember having a snack at the Wheelus Air Force Officer's Club after we arrived in the evening of August 26, 1960. We were taken to a temporary quarters or BOQ (Bachelor Officers' Quarters). A new acquaintance, Larry Grimm, an elementary teacher, and I walked along the shore of the Mediterranean Sea, right outside of our quarters. We looked across the Mediterranean and commented that Italy was to the north of us and how exciting it was to be in an area with Europe not too far away.

I would spend many days during that fall semester walking along the shores of the Mediterranean Sea, with its warm water so inviting. I spent many afternoons on through September and early October swimming or lying in the sun. What a fabulous place to enjoy my third full year of teaching.

The trips to town, whether on a bus, a taxi or riding with some teacher who had already acquired an automobile, were exciting in themselves. The native Libyans were not all that friendly to Americans at that time.

I, who expected to complete a full year in Tripoli, immediately ordered a 1960 Volkswagen that did not arrive until about mid-October. I demanded an automobile from the local Volkswagen distributor because they did not deliver my car within the 2-week period. They loaned me an old red MG sports car and I at least had transportation. I had some good times squiring around beautiful Italian ladies that fall. Someway I met Moslems, Jews, and Italians who lived in the area. I went to several parties, revealed to me by my Volkswagen salesman, a Jewish, Italian and Arabic speaking nice young man. He always seemed to have a good-looking lady near him.

It was fortuitous that I looked up a friend of mine who was a pre-geology student at Arkansas A & M College before he attended the University of Arkansas in Fayetteville, Arkansas where he obtained his degree in geology. His name was Badir Al Refai, and I knew him from classes when attending Arkansas A & M College. We spoke often and he told me of his relatives in the Middle East. His home was Kuwait and his uncle, according to Badir, was in the oil business and doing quite well.

I was invited to his house in Tripoli and since he was familiar with the people of the area and the culture, it gave me an advantage since most of the teachers had little or no contact with the Arabic world. One of the things I remember, distinctly, about Badir was that he complained about the way the American technicians mistreated the Libyan workers around the oilrigs. He said they chastised and cursed the laborers in a demeaning way.

Badir, whom I remember as a polite and gentile sort of person, was a perfect host when I visited his home. He had an American wife whom he met in Arkansas and they were married in the United States. They came to Libya, as a geologist on his first assignment for an oil company based in Tripoli. They had a little boy, about five years of age and he adored the beautiful, dark haired, brown eyed child. The boy did, however, have the run of the house and Badir and his wife seemed to lay down very few guidelines for the boisterous, energetic, and somewhat wild kid.

I learned, some years later, through correspondence, that his wife died quite young. She was a lovely, somewhat taller lady than Badir, but expressed a great deal of love and respect for Badir. Both, of course adored their little boy. I lost track of Badir, much to my disappointment, several years after the correspondence through several letters that we exchanged while I was teaching in Ramstein, Germany from 1961-1966.

One thing that Badir did solicit from me while I lived in Tripoli, was merchandise from the commissary. Things were much cheaper than on the Libyan economy and there were certain American products his wife wanted for their household. Since I had the privileges and didn't use the commissary often, I was glad to accommodate him and his wife.

The Alrefais, if I remember correctly, bought a house while on assignment there. Many of the American oil companies left Libya in the 1960s, after the takeover by of the country by Muammar Qadhafi. King Idris was overthrown and the American government ceased to have the good relations previously exuded with the Idris monarchy.

I immediately began classes in Arabic, after my second week in Tripoli and found my teacher to be quite aggressive, traditional, and quite dictatorial. Actually, he turned me off to really getting into the language, but I stayed with him until I was transferred to Germany in late January 1961. The instructor often put me on the spot with verbal expressions, in Arabic, that I had problems with, and I was somewhat embarrassed me in front of the other teachers. Today I would not be because new languages are difficult. Being a country bumpkin from Arkansas, I was somewhat shy trying to unsuccessfully pronounce words unfamiliar to me.

I also exposed myself to the local culture as much as could be expected, by frequenting Arabic restaurants as well as the many Italian restaurants in the city of Tripoli. I learned to enjoy the dish called Couscous, the staple grain crop accompanying most meals of lamb and chicken.

We learned that the term "Sadiki," meaning friend in Arabic. This term was often used about the base when the hired Muslim waiters served us at the Officer's Club or NCO Club. Sometimes the term was almost hypocritical because we all knew the Moslem workers were not really our friends, but the U. S. Air Force pilots and civilian workers did treat them quite well. I thought the Muslim workers were very friendly, no doubt because of a decent pay scale that the American government provided them.

The resentment of Americans driving their big cars brought over, either by the American Government or oil companies, was quite noticeable as one drove around the Tripoli and its surrounding areas.

The new Volkswagen I purchased from the local Tripoli VW dealer finally arrived so I turned in my old MG sports car loaner. The new VW provided me the opportunities to visit the local areas and drive about Tripoli and along the coast to the east of the city and to the west of the city. One ancient Roman area to the east provided us with a beautiful ruin, and also the area to the west of the city provided another ruin. One was the ancient Roman, to the east, ruin known as Leptis Magna and the other, to the west, known as Sabratha. Both were beautiful examples of archaeological splendor and I often visited them, picking up ancient Roman coins, or buying them from some of the Libyan citizens who hung around the areas just for the purpose of selling the coins to the tourists, the teachers, or military from Wheelus Air Base.

Tripoli was, in my opinion, a beautiful city along the Mediterranean coast! It was exciting just living there and I was making the most of my tour. I even took some of the lady teachers on visits to the two Roman ruins on weekends, but usually after I did my substitute teaching at the local oil school on Saturday. In the suburbs on the west side of Tripoli there was an oil school for the children of the geologists who worked for the oil companies. They were great children to teach and came from caring and responsible parents. The school only went to about the 7th grade, then after that age they went to private schools in Italy, or perhaps Switzerland.

Fortunately I knew the director of the oil school who was a very nice person and called me every Friday to teach on Saturday, since the Dependent Schools did not have school on Saturday. I taught there as a means of making extra money, and it was a diversion and an enjoyable way to make extra money.

Actually my students of biology at Wheelus High School were fine students and most of them were children of Air Force personnel. We had some students from oil company employees since the oil company school only went to about seventh grade. They were all great kids and I loved working at the 10th grade level of high school since I had all only biology classes.

Later I was challenged about my credential since I was short of biology credits and my background, at that time was mostly general science, with a minimum number of credits in biological science. Since the school was going through an accreditation with the North Central Association, I ran into a problem, and it was a big problem.

I was too short of credits to be teaching biology and the parents wanted a replacement with a teacher who had a stronger biology background, and that is eventually what they got. There was a teacher at Ramstein Junior High who had about 90 hours in biology since he had prepared for medicine before deciding to teach, and he was the man the school wanted me to swap places with. His name, Vince Nava and he was from New York City. We were asked to exchange places. He was to come, after the first semester, to Tripoli and I was to go to Ramstein Air Base in Germany, a prime, excellent assignment!

I agreed to take the re-assignment and Vince, though he balked, finally accepted. He, however, chose to drive his new Volkswagen to Tripoli, using a ferry boat from the boot of Italy. They administration, out of Wiesbaden, wanted us to even agree on swapping cars but Vince wouldn't hear of it. I sold my car to the local librarian, who paid me what I paid for the car.

While in Tripoli, I took advantage of sightseeing, dating young Italian beauties, and one especially charming British secretary named Gloria. I almost fell in love with her but did keep my senses, just squiring her around base parties, and various parties in and around Tripoli.

Gloria became my steady woman and I never longed for sex as long as I remained in Tripoli. I had some difficulty getting accustomed to her somewhat arrogant British ways, but she finally became accustomed to my Arkansas down home tendencies and we finally got to know each other well enough to enjoy sleeping together quite frequently.

The days in Tripoli, after October, were really beautiful, and cooled down from the 100+ degrees Fahrenheit temperature. The date season, in September and early October brought on many flies, which became a nuisance, especially at the outdoor restaurants. In late October and later it cooled off enough to eliminate most of them. Many of the restaurants were Italian and provided the typical European Mediterranean experiences of eating. The contrast of Tripoli to all I had know in the United States, with the absence of European atmosphere, provided me a warmth difficult to describe. One has to actually be abroad to capture the experience of breaking out of the bonds of our secure and sometimes provincial existence in the United States.

The "feeling" of escaping the heavy chains that bind us to home, family, and job, is somewhat difficult to verbalize, but once a person, especially a younger person, feels it, smells it, and bathes in it, that "abroad" experience is to say the least, exuberating and transcending! I do not know how it would be, at my present age, to suddenly have the experience of being transported to another culture, especially as contrasting as that of North Africa, after existing in a world of work and family for fifty years or so.

I have a friend, quite successful, who has conformed to the working and professional world, along with his wife, never been outside of the United States, but has sent all 4 of his offspring abroad. One of them visited me in Germany in about 1980. All of them adored the experience of going abroad.

He and his wife, unfortunately, have not had the European experience but I think we might do it someday, and with my ties to Germany, I would love to be their guide!

I have one distinct message I wish to convey in this book, from my experience abroad. The message is that the experience was quite positive, and that I would give it, on a scale of 1 to 10, a 10+. Also, if one has just a little "wanderlust," and the opportunity to work abroad comes into one's perspective, by all means, grasp it! I have so often heard, especially from teachers, "I would like to try working abroad, with the military or an oil school, and have so often thought about it." These types, no doubt, have that element of "wanderlust," but I am certain that they will never make it because they have not already tried the experience at that early point in their lives when it would have been most feasible and relatively easy to do. Single teachers and professionals, especially, have a great opportunity for abroad assignments.

As the fall semester of 1960 moved toward winter holidays, I explored the ruins to the east and west of Tripoli, took rides, in my Volkswagen, on the back roads of Tripoli. I ventured out to sites south of the city and explored the scant and few villages in the area. I was sometimes accompanied by lady teachers and explored the caves and shorelines around Tripoli. One of the significant things I noticed about the very poor Arabic speaking Libyans was their tendency to put their hands out and beg.

In the parking areas of downtown Tripoli those willing to assist us in parking were always there, and had their hands out for a tip. In the hinterlands, beggars came out of every cave, nook and cranny to beg! There were many caves in the outer areas of Tripoli, and people actually lived in them. The country was one of the poorest of the Arabic countries at that time. I have not researched the economic status of Libya since King Idris was overthrown in a coup by Colonel Muammar al-Qaddafi in 1969. There are some indications that he (Khadafi) wants to get back into the graces with American interests.

I learned to enjoy the Libyan restaurants with their grilled lamb and chicken, along with the great dishes of Couscous, the staple grain meal of the Libyans. If only I could have spoken Arabic, I am sure the experience of Libya would have been an even more invigorating experience. The contrast of living in Libya to later living in Germany, where I became involved in the language and culture, due to the longevity of my exposure, is quite dramatic. The insecurity I endured, at that time, in Libya made the comparison between Germany and Libya extreme. Germany provided secure settings with pro-Americans while Libya provided a feeling of uncertainty. Although Libya had a natural beauty but unsanitary conditions compared to Germany, it was still exciting living there.

I bought my first camera toward the end of my stay in Libya. I think I bought it in early January (3 weeks before departure for Germany) and was just getting to know about ASA or Din settings (speeds of the film), f-stop settings and shutter speeds. It was not until I transferred to Germany that I purchased a nice Canon range finder type camera, then later got into single lens reflexes, and started accumulating photos of my experiences abroad. But the mental pictures one logs in one's memory bank are the ones that trigger that desire to either return to certain areas or expand the processes of cultural contact and in various countries. Writing is certainly an adroit manner of mental reflection or vicarious revisitation!

One of the destinations I had planned to visit while living in Libya was Egypt. I anticipated and planned a spring trip to that country during the spring holidays on the Dependent School calendar for 1961. But the trip never evolved. My full school year experience to be, in Libya, turned out to be a one-semester experience and my anticipated stay of one year faded away once I learned about my forthcoming transfer to Germany.

CHAPTER 3

Saying Goodbye to Tripoli

I was just getting settled in Tripoli when I learned of my forthcoming transfer to Germany. I auditioned for parts in U. S. Embassy plays, and was even selected for a part but because of my forthcoming transfer to Ramstein, Germany, I never completed the task. I also substituted for the Oil School, and made friends, Libyan, American, and other Continentals during my brief five-month stay in Libya. But then I learned of my reassignment so I knew the friendships would soon be diminishing and other friends were to be made on the Continent.

The beautiful sands blowing in from the south during the hot warm desert winds captivated my mind. The Libyan Desert, the date palms, camels, women with veils, and men in their long woolen robes, enchanted me to an expanded state of psychedelic ecstasy! The wandering gazelles, spitting camels, and bazaars outside the base were proof of my existence in a strange land. The male Libyans gazing at my women friends as we drove by or walked about the stores in downtown Tripoli elevated me to a state of another existence. I really loved the exotic culture so different from my previous, somewhat provincial background.

All these things crowded my mind, pushing at a possible override of my brain, and my unconscious mind shouting, "I want out of here, this is too extreme for this Arkansas lad!" But my mind worked in another way. Had I have stayed the full year in Libya, I might have been enticed to visit another country in the Arabic world. These were countries such as Algeria, Morocco, and Egypt also extremely contrasted to my home in the United States. But the transfer, coming up in January, to Germany, provided me with an "escape," from this very poor and primitive setting, though I, personally enjoyed its extreme contrast to my past. The forthcoming transfer was an opportunity, and one, most of my colleagues thought was a great one, to move on to one of my target countries I had planned to live in during my overseas adventure. I had always preconceived, mentally, Spain, Germany, or France, as target countries.

The Libyan experience was just not long enough for me. I still wanted to delve in the Arabic language, mix more with the Libyans, and explore the areas to the east such as Egypt to the east or Tunisia, Algeria and Morocco to the west. Many of the teachers took drives to Tunisia, immediately to the west of Libya, during the Thanksgiving holiday, and many planned such trips for the forthcoming spring of 1961. The teachers would load up with Jerry Cans (large military containers) of gasoline and strike out along the Mediterranean coast so they could visit Algeria. I could not make such a trip because I was being transferred to the Continent!

One of the very interesting experiences I had while teaching biology for the high school in Tripoli was the visit Dr. Ochsner made to the medical hospital on Wheelus Air Base in Tripoli. He was the first physician to make a study of smoking, in the 1950s, of 10,000 deceased veterans. He was the first research doctor to bring the conclusions that smoking 1 pack of cigarettes a day for twenty years, would put 86 people in any group of a hundred, into the early stages of lung cancer. Other fascinating discoveries were made in the study, such as filters made little difference, the closer to the end of the cigarette one smoked, the more tar deposit on the lungs, and the tars were the carcinogens that caused the cancer. Smoking among young people is begun, in about 80% of the cases, because of social and peer pressure. He was a fascinating lecturer and he made the statement that he would never allow any of his practicing interns at the Ochsner Clinic in New Orleans to smoke while on duty.

This just a side issue that I bring up, and it illuminates the military. The American military because of its worldwide presence often keeps up with what is going on in the world. The military schools, in my opinion, were overall, better than most of the schools in the United States. Of course the select group of students and money allocations from the U. S. Congress kept their status up. The overseas schools, as an American model are the best, in my opinion, and I have taught in both public school settings; at home and abroad. I was beginning to get a taste of what teaching would be like in a coming twenty-five year career of teaching and serving as an educator abroad.

Another insight I gained while living in Libya was one as to why we Americans were not loved a lot by the Libyans. I did not have much contact with the oil company personnel, except for my weekend teaching and meeting some of the oil conglomerate administrators who came to the base to discuss the uncovered Lady Be Good B-24 that was lost in the Libyan Desert during World War II.

Badir Al Refai, the student with whom I attended college at the University of Arkansas, Monticello, Arkansas, enlightened me quite a bit about how the American oil personnel treated the local Libyans in the oil fields in the Libyan Desert. He told me that the technicians treated the Libyan workers badly. Actually Badir, himself, a professional and a geologist, was a native of Kuwait and had a lot of rich uncles and brothers in that country. Badir, previously mentioned in this book, invited me, on numerous occasions, to his home where I enjoyed some great dinners.

Badir did not overburden me with demands to shop in the commissary. He only asked me a couple of times and I was glad to oblige, especially since I had some nice meals at his house. It was an insight into a household that was at least over 50% Arabic. It was also a good chance to mix with a family that spoke the native language. I reiterate this experience because he turned out to be a vital contact while I was living in Libya. Had I have remained the full year, I would have utilized his knowledge of the language and culture even more extensively. We got along quite well in the university and socialized quite a bit in college, so his friendship had already been established in the United States.

I learned that he was in Libya via letters to my friends back in Arkansas. He lived in a very lovely villa and was not far from Wheelus Air Base so visiting his wife and him was quite convenient, and a great experience.

One of the scary experiences I had while ambling around the city of Tripoli one Saturday morning was to run into a mass of about 200 Libyan protesters. They were supporting Nasser, then leader of Egypt and whenever a world political even caused disruption, the Arabic people were up in arms. I do not remember the specific event during that fall of 1960, but something got these people aroused and I, fortunately, ducked into a restaurant and bar before I was overrun by these rather distraught protesters. After the mass of demonstrators marched past the restaurant and bar, I came out after the street looked safe.

I often heard from some of my Libyan friends that the United States always extended more foreign aid to Israel than to the Arabic countries. The Jews were often cited, and somewhat disdainfully, when they were discussing international affairs, and this was quite often. I listened to their pleas, but I as only one citizen, did not have extensive insight into the political intricacies involved in such world events. Today, however, we are learning that oil dependence has certainly highlighted the Arabic speaking oil producers of the Middle East! In fact, the 1991 war over Iraq's invasion of Kuwait, and the political intrigues still existing between the United States and Iraq are complex and perennial to say the least.

As I write this book, we look at the success of the military in driving out the Saddam Hussein regime in Iraq. Our problems, in settling the country and getting it to be run with a viable, pro-United States regime, still exist.

The Libyans in 1960 often looked at the oil workers and the American military, because they were such poor people, rather enviously, especially with our many automobiles and villas about Tripoli. The workers on base got their eyes full as the American military and civilians threw their money around rather freely. It is no wonder that they did look upon us with some envy, and often disdain!

I was to experience a contrast in culture when I transferred to Germany because the German people never envied, in my opinion, the Americans, they just wanted to again rise to the same affluence as we! The Germans were hard working, festival loving, and extremely progressive toward rebuilding their society.

I now reflect back on my acceptance of the location and assignment I had at Wheelus High School, and see it as a dynamic experience! The school, if my memories are correct, was over 900 students in grades 7-12. My new assignment to soon come up was in a junior high but it happened to be one of the best schools in Europe. I did not prefer the junior high because students at this age level are not my preference in secondary teaching. The students at Ramstein Junior in 1961-1966 proved to be exceptional in behavior and performance, however!

The fall in Tripoli quickly turned into winter and a very mild winter compared to what one found on the continent of Europe. Wheelus Air Base was a base used to provide logistics for air squadrons flying down from

Europe, mostly Germany. The weather in North Africa provided sunshine almost 365 days a year and beautiful flying weather.

I met several pilots whom I had known in various parts of the world and who were flying out of such U. S. Airbases as Spangdahlem, Bitburg, and Ramstein, Germany. I think the base was also utilized by the Canadian Air Force. The pilots, married or not, enjoyed the company of the young women, mostly elementary teachers. I do not remember how long the tours were but I think they were short TDY (temporary duty) assignments from various units in the United States. Some of the Air Force pilots were stationed in Germany, Italy, France, or England for 2-year assignments at that time.

One of the things I do specifically remember about my stay in Libya was the lack of fresh milk. We were restricted, or at least warned in our briefing, not to drink or eat milk products. I think I did use the cream in my coffee downtown but did not drink milk. The bacteria count allowed per milliliter by the Americans was much lower than that in the Libyan society. There was the danger of tuberculosis and from what were told by the base medical personnel, there were many cases of tuberculosis in that area.

The pilots would often bring several cartons of fresh milk from the commissaries in various bases in Germany, France, or Italy, or England. Once in awhile I would have students whose parents were active military and could get the milk. The commissary milk at Wheelus was the powdered milk mixed with water and did not have the taste of good dairy milk.

We also had to be very cautious about the salads, especially any leafy type vegetables because of the spread of amoebic dysentery. Any leafy vegetables or salads had to be washed in a Chlorine or Clorox solution. Tomatoes were safe to eat because of the low pH, which can kill any bacteria or virus in the fruit. The high concentration of acid in the tomato keeps it safe from the various microbes.

The ice cream, especially from the Italian type ice cream establishments, was very tempting and I do recall eating that several times. Luckily I never contracted any disease while I was aware. Perhaps I contracted some bacterial dysentery now and then but never anything serious.

We were also cautioned to be very careful if eating at the local Libyan homes, because of the possibility of contracting various diseases from their foods. My contacts, however, were mostly, were with Badir Al Refai, my Kuwaiti friend with whom I attended university.

The Libyan friends whom I had become acquainted with were members of the Libyan Army and I remember one was a major and the other was actually a colonel. Both were very young and they must have had close contacts with influential friends of the then King Idris.

It was quite interesting how sometimes the Libyan friends would walk down the street and even hold your hand in friendship, a custom that certainly does not exist in our country, except perhaps with men who are gay. This is just not a custom American men are familiar with. But it did not bother me since I knew it was acceptable and I went along with it because the man, married, and a Libyan military officer did not upset me when he did this on several occasions.

I remember one of the officers, the colonel, later moved to Germany, and I heard he married a German lady, after Muammar Qadhafi took hold of the country in the 1969. I tried to contact this gentleman but could never find him. I heard he settled around Kaiserslautern but never found him.

It was also quite interesting that the U. S. Air Force provided King Idris with a plane, plush DC-4, reciprocating engine plane, in which he could be flown, for his wife and him on shopping or medical visits to the Continent of Europe at his beckoning. Military personnel told me this. The plane was also used to fly in diplomats or even the North Central Accreditation group that came down from Germany to evaluate the Dependent Schools on Wheelus Air Base.

I happened to have flown in that plane when coming back from my visit to France, Switzerland, and Germany during the winter holidays in December and January 1960-61. It is also the plane I flew up to Germany on when I got my transfer to Germany in late January 1961.

I had the good fortune of meeting Dr. Joseph Mason while he was on his pre-NCA inspection in about November 1960. He later became Director of Dependent Schools worldwide. He and I became well acquainted while I was teaching in Libya and I later encountered him while teaching in Italy, the Netherlands, then again in Germany where he had his headquarters in Karlsruhe.

I never really knew the value of knowing this gentleman until he later gave me an opportunity to go into administration. He talked with me about going into administration in 1968 and I should have taken him up on the offer. But my dedication to teaching in my early years of teaching was quite strong and I loved kids and being in the classroom.

The mobility that teaching provided me was great because it gave me the opportunity to be in such a place as Libya, then later in different places in Europe. Teaching is a profession that provides many opportunities and all one has to do today is store files on a laptop computer and go! At that time one had to carry around, perhaps, various teaching aides. I never had a lot of these, was very adaptive, and also utilized the various science programs provided by the Dependent Schools, especially after the mid-1960s.

The day in January, immediately after I returned from my rest and recuperation trip to Germany and Switzerland for winter holidays. I was to report to Ramstein Junior High for a general science assignment. I did not take long to pack up my few belongings that all fit into about 2 footlockers. I took a couple of large travel bags on the plane with me and sent my hold baggage to Larry Stell, c/o Ramstein Junior High, Ramstein Air Base.

The baggage arrived in less than thirty days, once I did arrive at Ramstein Air Base, Germany, and I was ready to utilize the few sports coats and long sleeved shirts I had but very few since I had accumulated a wardrobe for Mediterranean wear.

I sold my 1960 Volkswagen (newly purchased) to the base librarian, a German lady, and said all of my good-byes to the very nice and friendly teachers at Wheelus Air Base. It did not take long to end my relationship with my British lady friend, Gloria, and she and I had already had some misunderstandings, many which, in my opinion emanated from her British arrogance. Maybe now that I am older, I would not have been so defensive about my provincial ways. Now, with a fluency in another language besides English and travels in many lands, I probably would have been more appealing and would have been more comfortable around this British beauty!

The sands of the desert were about to be left behind me. The veils of the women, the robes of the men, the camels, the caravans, the Mediterranean, and the date palms of beautiful Libya would be an indentation in my memory bank. The contrast of culture so extreme and different from a lad out of the depth of Arkansas would soon shift to that which I originally wanted-the heart of Europe!

Before leaving this chapter, I would like to reflect on an overview from Search Arab Net, describing a short account of Qaddafi's rise to power in Libya: "In the late 1960s anti-western feeling gradually spread from Egypt into Libya, and the country became politically unstable once more. The path of Libya's history was radically altered in 1969 by a military coup which successfully overthrew the monarchy. Led by a group of young army officers under Colonel Muammar al-Qaddafi, the country was re-established as a republic and became known as the Libyan Arab Republic.

The country welcomed Colonel Qaddafi as a strong nationalist leader. He immediately embarked on a bold series of programs designed to establish himself as the focus of a united Arab world. Alcohol was banned from Libya, all foreign languages were vetoed in official business, banks were nationalized and all private sector economic activities were abolished. Oil resources were also nationalized, and trade embargoes were encouraged against those nations that supported Israel.

Qaddafi's Green Book set out his ideas on Arab socialism, declaring that democracy was an unworkable system. In its place he set up people's committees in all administrative districts, and these committees reported annually to a General People's Congress.

Qaddafi made concerted efforts towards Arab unity, with attempts to merge Libya with a succession of countries. These included Egypt, Syria, Chad, Morroco, and Algeria. Although a federation was formed in 1971 between Egypt, Libya and Syria, in order to strengthen their military position against Israel, this was later abandoned, and all similar attempts at unity likewise failed."

At the time Qaddafi took over the country, I was teaching in the Netherlands with a NATO 4 Nation School, AFCENT (Allied Forces Central Europe). My memories of Libya had begun to wane but the beauty I found there was almost surreal because of the beauty of the warm desert land along the Mediterranean!

CHAPTER 4

Ramstein, Germany (1961-1966)

The snow was at least 2 feet high as I trudged up the street from my stop at the office at Ramstein Junior High School and introduced myself to the principal of the rather large junior high school. If my memory is correct, its enrollment was pushing 900 students and that is a large junior high. Its grade group was 7th through 9th and the ninth grade does provide the freshman year of high school credits.

I had taken a train from Wiesbaden, Germany, after my DC-4 flight with Dr. Joseph Mason and his evaluation team that remained a week at Wheelus High School and Elementary School. Our stop at the fascinating city of Marseilles, France because of a faulty compass was most interesting. I often wonder if those pilots do not look for excuses to remain overnight at interesting cities, especially in the overseas arena.

The green pines, illuminated by an abundance of snow, enhanced the lovely setting of Ramstein Air Base, located in the State of Rheinland-Pfalz, one of the states of West Germany. "What a contrast I thought," after trudging the 3 blocks or so to the Officer's Club where I had dinner and ran into a couple of teachers to whom I introduced myself.

The teachers, I thought, were fat and happy, settled down already for over a semester into the school year of 1960-61. They all had their officer quarters on base and it was only a stone's throw to the Ramstein Officer's Club. The base had three theatres, about 3 restaurants, and the Ramstein Officer's Club; two of them existed if my memory is correct. The NCO Club (Non Commissioned Officers) was great and Ramstein had one of the most active Rod and Gun Clubs in Europe. There were, I believe, two Rod and Gun Clubs and the one on the north base is where I spend many afternoons after school drinking beer with a group of close knit teachers, mostly male.

It was in this Rod and Gun Club where I would study the famous German hunting system and acquire my Jäger Brief, the Hunter's Diploma, before beginning a twenty-year of hunting around Germany and France. I fell in love with the methodical concept of the German Abschuss Plan (German Conservation Plan) for balancing the game with the food supply on any plot of land.

I learned to shoot a high powered rifle for the deer in the area and chose the .270 Remington rifle and eventually would begin to use the .308 Winchester rifle. I also got into the beautifully balanced over and under .12 gauge Winchester 101 guns and was to find they were a work of art in hunting partridge, European hare, pheasant, and duck in the Rhine River area.

The social ramifications of hunting with the very elite hunters of Germany could extend into a book and the contacts I made through hunting turned out to be the exposure I needed to meet many Germans.

My five years in Ramstein, Germany from January 1961 until August 1966 turned out to be one of the richest tours I could ever have perceived. I married my German wife, Brigitte, whom I admire and respect today, even though we divorced in 1986. She and I are still close and visit each other quite often. Fortunately she is splitting her time between Austin, Texas and Bad Kreuznach, Germany. Her energy is inexhaustible and there her personality and charm took us through many memorable experiences.

Ramstein Air Base proved to be a facility that provided any necessities a family needed. There were a couple of Quartermaster gasoline stations on base and the Esso as well as the Quartermaster Gasoline coupons were also available. In 1961 gasoline cost about 9 U.S. cents per gallon and about 14 U. S. cents for the Esso coupons that could be used all over Germany. We could also get the coupons for France and Italy, and Spain since we had bases in these countries.

When I arrived at Ramstein Air Base, the first thing I did was buy an old Volkswagen and began to wander to the local places first and then drive to surrounding areas. I would visit Luxembourg, France, and closer areas of Germany, such as Stuttgart, Nuremberg, Munich, Frankfurt, Bitburg, Mainz, Mannheim, Heidelberg, and Wiesbaden. They were all interesting cities and the drives on weekends were not too far.

I fell in love with Germany almost immediately. I had been in the country for a short time when I had to depart from Wiesbaden Air Base on my way to Tripoli, returning from my winter vacation in early January 1961.

I picked up a dictionary and two Jerry cans (large military gasoline cans) to sustain longer journeys so we could use the Quartermaster gasoline and stretch our trips out even to Austria and Switzerland. I explored every nook and cranny in the immediate surrounding areas of southwestern Germany, got over into Strassbourg and Metz, France, then later on to Paris, France. What a life! Europe was mine and I was going to enjoy every bit that was available to me.

I visited cathedrals, medieval cities, shopping areas, Hitler's parade grounds in Nuremberg, and beautiful castles and forests in the areas surrounding Ramstein. I traced the Wein Strasse, took cruises on the Rhine, and explored the lovely city of Aachen and the Ardiennes Forest.

Today, when I return to Germany, enjoy the great white wines and fantastic beers, I feel very much at home. The German foods, rich in their great dishes of venison, wild boar, pheasant, schnitzels, pot roasts, and fish make me hungry just writing about them.

When I first settled in at the BOQ (Bachelor Officer Quarter) at Ramstein Air Base, I soon learned to drive through the back woods and find my way into Ramstein Village, adjacent to the base, on the southwest side. I learned of a Gasthaus called Lilli's and soon learned from a very good science teacher and friend, Hank, that the food was cheap and the "pop top" bottles of beer cost only about 50 German Pfennig or about 25 U. S. cents. What a wonderful discovery! I learned to drive the non-synchronized old Volkswagen without shifting, especially when I had had about 3 bottles of the very strong beer.

I soon learned that Kartoffel Soupe (potato soup) and wurst, either bratwurst or knackwurst with potato salad were excellent meals and unusually cheap. I also began my immediate German lessons and learned the niceties in the German language quickly.

I immediately went to evening school 3 nights a week, taking private German lessons from the local Berlitz Schule in Kaiserslautern, only about 10 kilometers from Ramstein Air Base. I asked for a private lady German instructor because I had become shy of dictatorial traditional men teachers from my experience down in Tripoli. The Arabic teacher seemed to be very autocratic and I thought, at that time, I did not have a propensity for languages. I was to learn later that this was not true and I took to languages; German and Italian (a later duty station) like a duck swimming in water.

I had the German lady teacher for about 2 months and eventually got shuffled to a man whom I found gracious and excellent, especially in his attack on the subjective, direct object, indirect object case, along with the genitive. He was excellent and I learned a lot from him about spoken German.

Later I started evening classes via the University of Maryland extension courses set up for the U. S. military and civilians living in Europe. The classes gave one the opportunity to build in languages and I eventually picked up 12 semester hours then when I returned to the United States (San Diego State and University of California, San Diego), I completed about 40 semester units, giving me a solid major in the German language.

The congeniality of the German people in the region of Rheinland-Pfalz, where I was living, appealed to me. I was to later find out the German people many differ in affability, seemingly, as one moved from one region to the other. I always found the northern Germans a little bit more stand offish and perhaps not as quick to carry on conversations, as in other areas.

I am a very outgoing person so meeting people for me is not a difficult task. Once I began to master the language I was less reticent to stand back and listen to opinions in everyday conversations. As I began to polish my conversation German, I readily engaged in conversation on most any occasion, especially in business relations related to my school work. I had contacts with visiting teachers or visited local German schools and readily spoke with the German Gymnasium, Realschule, or Grundschule teachers.

Most of the base personnel, officer club employees, BOQ cleaning ladies, Base Exchange employees, and even some German traffic directors on base or at the gate, were Germans. The Americans provided a significant number of positions for the German citizenry.

One thing that enchanted me when I arrived at Landstuhl, Germany, near Ramstein Airbase, was the old beautiful train station, the local restaurants, old but quite good, with great wine and beer. The merchants were always very congenial and happy to sell a Bier, a Bratwurst, Brot (bread), or Goulasch Suppe to an American.

One of my teacher friends, a very liberal social studies teacher in the junior high where I taught often came by my BOQ room and prodded me out of my room to go to a local German restaurant. There we would enjoy a good meal of Wildschwein (wild boar) or Reh (venison), or even a great

Wienerschnitzel. The true Wienerschnitzel is veal breaded and fried. It was relatively inexpensive in the 1960s but if one buys it today, get ready to pay possibly $15 or more for a good one.

It was not until the spring of 1961, possibly March or April, that I met my future wife to be-Brigitte von Jagow. She was by all rights, a blue blood and evidence was readily available related to her ancestors of von Jagows, one of them being a World War I Finance Minister of Germany, or some very high position similar to that position.

When I met my wife, proceeded to fall in love and propose to her after returning to the United States for continued studies toward graduate studies in sociology at Vanderbilt Peabody University in Nashville, Tennessee, in the summer of 1961. I contacted her when I returned from the United States in late August and found out her mother wanted her to return to Kiel. Brigitte was working for a dentist because she had studied to be a dental technician/assistant.

I dated her up through September 1961, when she then returned to Kiel to work and be close to her mother. I knocked around the base for a few weeks and missed her love and tender care, so decided to go after her in early November o 1961. I brought her back after getting the lower part of a house in a nearby village of Bann that was just outside of Landstuhl, and only a few kilometers from the Air Base.

I moved Brigitte into the house, one heated with oil that I had to bring in in Jerry cans so this proved to be a difficult situation. I lived with Brigitte through the winter, took her to Switzerland during the winter vacation because by then I had purchased another new Volkswagen, a 1961 model similar to the one I had in Libya. I loved those little Volkswagen Beetles because they were so well built and pulled through the snow like a snowplow.

After my fiancée suffered a couple of grueling head colds and provided me the comfort of keeping house tidy, and cooking for me, up through the spring of 1962, then returning to her mother in Kiel, Germany, I began to miss her company and eating meals alone.

I confronted her mother in Kiel and told her I wanted her daughter's hand in marriage. We got married in June of 1962 and eventually moved into warmer quarters in officer's housing on base. This proved to be great in that the heat was a non cost item, as well as the quarters.

One of the advantages of living abroad, especially as an employee of the Department of Defense, is the non taxed housing. Even if one lives off base and is given a housing allowance, at that time $300 to $400/month, it is tax-free. We did not utilize off base housing again until September 1966 when we moved to Pordenone, Italy, where I taught in the Aviano Air Base Junior High/High School.

The great thing I liked about Ramstein Air Base, Germany, even on base housing, was the short distance to my work and many of my evening German classes were at the junior high where I worked. I was close to the on base German post office so this made it convenient for my wife to send her mother care packages that were quite frequent.

Also, during the spring, Thanksgiving, and winter vacations, my car, a larger American automobile by 1962, would be filled with turkeys, coffee, many alcoholic beverages, cigarettes, and any other expensive items to supply the very poor mother of my wife. Unfortunately Brigitte's mother had to divorce her husband, the father of a family of seven, after the war. There was some financial advantage of his not staying with her, according to my wife. It was probably because she could only exist with a stipend from the welfare system of West Germany.

I actually loved "Mutti" because we got along about 85% or the time but sometimes did not see eye to eye when she made too many monetary demands on Brigitte and me.

My salary, at that time, was relatively good compared to the German teacher with a position similar to mine. I had base housing, cheap gasoline, inexpensive PX and commissary living. I had the good life and my frugal wife could really stretch a U. S. dollar or a German Mark.

We utilized all the fantastic facilities about the 10,000 personnel base of Ramstein Air Base. I could not believe the base, one of the largest in Germany, was so huge, but it was. There was a South and a North Base and we utilized the many restaurants and clubs, and even had German family in during New Years celebrations because of the great entertainment and low cost. We often had Brigitte's brother, Detlef, and his wife or her sister Edith, who was married to a French Colonel, Gilbert Poitier. All of her sisters and brothers were like family to me and gave me the opportunity to exercise my German in a fashion that would be related to the most extensive language lab existing in the universe.

Ramstein Air Base, even used today for logistics in receiving military from all over the world remains one of the most dynamic and modern facilities of the U. S. Military anywhere in the world. I often returned there, even when I was stationed outside Germany because of the great facilities. One could buy car parts, food of any kind, hunting products (rod and gun clubs), clothes, and any other needs of the family.

It was always my worry that with such a concentration of personnel, over 10,000, the Russians could have well targeted it and really done some damage to the U. S. Forces during the Cold War.

Our stay in the Ramstein Air Base area from 1961 to 1966 was certainly five years of easy living. My wife began to work on her English and I began to have formal studies in German. The location was superb and one of the best and most modern duty stations I have ever lived on. It gave the opportunity to expand my language in a formal mode and mix with doctors, dentists, and other teachers. It was truly a Golden Ghetto!

CHAPTER 5

Travel to the German Villages

The stay in Ramstein, Germany provided me the opportunity to really get out into the local villages, even before I met my wife to be. I drove my old Volkswagen during my first three months with a high level of energy and a strong desire to explore the villages and small towns of Southwest Germany.

There were castles in almost every small "Dorf" or "Stadt" in Rheinland-Pfalz. A German "Dorf" is like our very small towns in population and a "Stadt" or city has to reach a certain number in Germany to be designated as such. The area was green, full of beautiful evergreens and hardwoods. The low rolling hills around Ramstein Air Base provided me with lovely areas to hike, and just drive my car and sightsee.

The aspect that really introduced me to the villages or small towns of the Rheinland-Pfalz State, were my newly adopted hunting skills. After I completed my hunting school, I got invitations to go hunting almost every weekend.

My friend, who was a teacher named Hank, introduced me to several hunters in the area so could go out into the woods and sit in the high seats in hopes of shooting a deer. The deer in that area were the Rehwild or Roe Deer (English name) and they weigh only about 30 to 35 lbs. They are, however, beautiful animals and about the tastiest venison I have ever eaten. "Wild," by the way, in German, refers to game in general.

The first deer I shot (Rehwild and a female) was actually on an organized hunt by the local forester who had Ramstein Air base under his jurisdiction. I was sitting in a high seat near the runway of Ramstein Airbase in the early spring, about March, of 1961, and I finally shot the deer at about 140 meters out. I was using my newly purchased .270 Remington bolt action rifle and had a mounted 4 X power scope. It was my first experience with a high powered rifle so it was a new hunting experience since I was accustomed to shooting deer with either slugs or double 0 buckshot in the U.S.

I, during my stay in Germany, was to explore many small villages in the region and enjoy the fascinating drive hunts so well organized by the German hunters. Safety is of utmost importance when hunting in Germany and one who carries a license must have hunter's insurance.

I remember one hunt I was invited to one Saturday in the fall of 1961 and there were about forty hunters and about fifteen of them were American military and civilians. We were near the Rhine River, near Speyer, Germany. It was a beautiful fall day and we were hunting in cornfields along the Rhine River basin with about 10 dogs working the fields as we moved across the fields with hunters on the end of the field and hunters on each side. I was moving with the line moving down the field and we hit an area where pheasant began to rise up in numbers that almost blackened the skies.

We were shooting for almost 20 minutes and before the end of the day we had almost 200 pheasant. There is not limit, the German hunter merely manages the pheasant and in most cases we were shooting the males, not the females. The farmer and owner of the land was a gentleman named Herr Hampsch. I shall never forget his name. He had several hundred acres to hunt on and some of the most beautiful fields for hunting I have ever seen.

The hunters had the all purpose German long hair and short hair dogs that worked beautifully with their owners having full control. One has never enjoyed hunting until one hunts in Germany, or at least it was terrific in the 1960s but from what I have read, with the population increase, the fields are diminishing in Germany. I do not know the status of hunting in East Germany since the reunification in 1989.

I have never felt so safe and secure as when hunting with the well-trained hunters. They are skilled in shooting and only a small percentage of the citizens hunt in Germany because hunting in that country is really for the elite. The training is intensive and sometimes takes a year or two to obtain the Hunter's diploma.

My life in the small village of Bahn, a "Dorf" with only several hundred people was also quite interesting. Every village or Germany will have a Jahrmarkt or a festival in the fall of the year. My ex wife, Brigitte cannot pass one of these and they are still prevalent in Germany.

There will be tables with tents in case of bad weather, tables with seats, fresh tap beer and various types of wine. There is always good food, usually schnitzel (pork or veal; more frequently pork today), bratwurst, bockwurst, the hard German rolls, and various types of soups.

If one wants to get the true flavor of Germany, I would suggest exploring the small towns or villages of Germany because one can get into the true experience of the great German festival. I, to my recollection, have never met a stranger in one of these great festivals and I have been in them in not only villages but in the cities from Kiel in the north to Munich in the south.

It is ironical but I have only been to the great "Oktoberfest" of Munich, Germany once and I think that was in about 1961, when I first came to Ramstein Air Base. There is really no need to attend this massive festival because of the wonderful and smaller festivals, sometimes beginning in late September on through October in Germany.

The small villages, no matter where one is, brings out the true spirit of the German mentality, that of enjoying getting together, drinking good beer and wine, and savoring good food! If Germans do not speak to you on the street in various towns or even villages, then when the festivals come about, they turn into gregarious, congenial, and outgoing people. Country or urban types, they are friendly at their festivals, and especially in the smaller villages.

I remember an occasion when I was driving from Trier, west of Ramstein, Germany and near Bitburg Air Base, Germany, on my way back to Ramstein, that I stopped in a small village for a festival. It was a small village but the food, wine and beer were excellent. Just getting into the German language, I soon learned that when one sits at a beer table, drinks his or her beer, eats a wonderful Bratwurst, then the German world has no strangers!

My spring went by rather quickly during my first semester at Ramstein Junior High. I liked the teachers, all trying to get along in German, and the students, for junior age, 7-9, turned out to be excellent and cooperating teachers. I thought teaching in such an environment was rather easy money. The school had about 900 students, rather large for a junior high but the time passed rather quickly and we often had visiting German teachers and classes close to the grade levels we had in our school. All the German teachers loved having us and were quick to invite us to their schools.

The immediate small towns or villages, such as Landstuhl and Ramstein, both towns and larger than villages, were close to the base and both had nice bakeries, Bier Stuben (taverns) and the people were friendly. It only took a whim in my mind to jump into my Volkswagen and drive to either Ramstein or Landstuhl. Landstuhl was a little larger and had a couple of Conditereis (coffee and cake shops) so there was a nice atmosphere if one wanted to drink coffee and eat delicious cakes. To this day I love the

German Kuchen (cakes) better in Germany than in most places in Europe. I would guess that Switzerland, Austria, and perhaps Scandinavia have excellent such coffee shops with oodles of whipped cream on the cakes.

The Villager, in Germany, a country with a 99% literacy rate, is not your general run of the mill country pumpkin. Usually the father has a job in a nearby large city and the wife is also working or staying home raising children. When I was there a high percentage of married women were raising their children. But as Germany began to build up its economy in the 1960s-1980s, more women worked, especially once the children could attend school. The German family really supports the small village festivals and enjoys the Saturday and Sunday festivals, especially in October.

The famous "Oktoberfest" is not only popular in Munich but almost in every German village, town, or city. I have not explored the eastern part of Germany since the fall of the Berlin Wall extensively, but I am sure this tradition was promulgated even more after the reigns of Communism and the control of East Germany under the Soviet Union. In my opinion, one of the biggest setbacks in modern history, was the control of Eastern Europe by the Soviets.

For the overseas worker, fortunate enough to live in Germany, I would highly advise visits to the hinterlands in Germany. Just driving through the very small towns and villages in Germany after an October rain, provides one with a touch, smell of the countryside that is almost impossible to describe in writing. It is a smell and feel one must experience by being there.

Conversation while you are sitting on the folding benches at a folding table provided by various breweries will not be difficult to get into. If you do not learn German, you will be motivated to do so. The Germans, with many commanding at least 2, other than their own, languages in school, will try to communicate with you in English. Some learn French and German as a second language, as my daughter did in the Gymnasium, highest secondary level school. But my daughter was fortunate enough to have me at home to help, if she needed it, in the English language. I could do very little toward French.

I remember the closeness we had with our neighbors in the very small village of Bann, near Landstuhl and Ramstein, in 1962. I got to know many of the families around me. One of the very negative things I can say about German neighbors is that, once they learn you are in anyway connected with the U. S. Forces, they will approach your landlord(s) and try to make a deal for cigarettes, coffee, or alcoholic products. That was the case in 1961-1980s, but does not know if it is so prevalent, or can be so prevalent, since the diminishing numbers of troops now stationed in Germany.

I was told by my teacher buddy, Hank, in 1961, that I would be approached by the Germans, especially the landlord, to buy certain items and the best solution was to merely give them such items as a gift, take no money, and they would no longer bother you. I did try this and it worked for awhile, until I left such interactions in the hands of my wife. How she took care of the inquiries was strictly in her hands.

Music is usually a big part of the village festivals, and almost all small towns and villages have their own bands. If they do not have a band, they will procure one for their week or 2 week festivals. The famous oom-pah-pah bands can strike up melodic Germanic tunes that will have you pounding on the wooden tables and talking with the Fräulein or Frau, or Herr, as though you had known them for years! Sometimes you will even get an invitation into their homes, once they know you are American. So many Germans have similarities with Americans, especially in the work mentality.

Once you can communicate in German, more doors will open and friends can be made. I would say that the utilization of the language, as in any country, is the most important factor related to overseas living. The only country I lived in and did not feel that learning the language, although

I did acquire a usage, was in the Netherlands. My home was so close to the German border, and the Dutch knew the German language, almost extensively, and I did not go into formal lessons as I did in Italy. I also felt that Dutch was not a major language and my target languages in Europe, if I had the opportunity would be German, Italian, French, and Spanish, and in that order for me personally.

Of the areas I lived in while in Germany, I always found the surrounding villages to be exceptionally friendly. I lived in Ramstein 1961-1966; Hagenbach 1971-1977 (both of these towns were in the State of Rheinland-Pfalz); and in Kitzingen (Ober Bayern-Upper Bavaria) August 1984-October 1984. Each area provided excellent festivals in the surrounding areas.

Actually Hagenbach, Germany was a village and was located very near the French border so its location gave me the opportunity to even wander across the border and enjoy some of the small village atmosphere of France. Their festivals, were usually wine and fish type events and most of the border people spoke German since it was in the Alscace area of France. Most of their events took place in the local restaurants and were not as concentrated; beer tents, and tables with the benches, as in Germany. The advantage of living near the French border was that I had the opportunity to ride my bicycle to France, only about 4 miles from my home in Hagenbach, and pick up French cheese and the long loaves of bread, along with the croissants.

In the local festivals, around Karlsruhe, located in Baden-Württemberg, I found the dialect to be quite delightful, with a tinge of the Black Forest slur. The people, as in Rheinland-Pfalz, were friendly and fun loving. I think the idea of fun loving must be prevalent throughout Germany. I did not, however, notice a rash of festivals in Northern Germany. The one big festival that I attended in Northern Germany was the "Kieler Woche," or Kiel Week that took place in the summer. It was a large city type festivity and people attended the sailing regattas from all over the world.

It was not unusual, especially when I was single, for some beautiful big busted Frau, married lady to grab my arm during the music and do the shaukel, melodic swinging from one side to the other on the benches. Many times I would catch those loving blue eyes of many a German Fräulein (single lady) or Frauen (married ladies and used for mature women), usually with their husbands on their sides, and think I had instantaneously fallen in love. I simply adore the feminine pulchritude of Germany. They are friendly, many so beautiful, and warm in conversation, especially when one speaks the language.

So many of the festivals, during some of the October festivals, have the tents set up because there is always a likelihood of rain. The bands with brass, accordions, drums, perhaps pianos, and melodic blasting music, can really get one into the festival spirit.

I remember when I first came to Germany and ran into an American officer describing the German mentality. "They are hard working but when it comes to festival time, they really know how to have fun!" I think this very well describes the German folk.

Actually, my wife and I created our own festival while I lived in Hagenbach, the village we lived in while I taught in Karlsruhe, Germany. I had many German hunting friends and created a list of about 50 hunting friends, through my immediate hunting friends and some of the landowners, both in the States of Rheinland-Pfalz and in Baden-Würtemberg. We managed to accumulate about 50 T-bone steaks, buy about 3 kegs of German beer and buy about 6 cases of beautiful German Rhine and Rheinland-Pfalz Wine. We had ample music from my stereo in my Kellar Bar (cellar bar) and also invited the traditional German horn blowers. Those are the hunters who blow horns as the game is laid out after the large drive hunts in Germany.

We had a house full of guests and managed to get the party down into the cellar area with an adjacent car port, with tables and benches set up to accommodate our guests. I wanted to impress the local Oberforstmeister (Head State Forester) from the Hagenbach area. He was there and was really the focus of the party. Sadly to say the gentleman is deceased, and I attribute it to the many of the cigarettes he smoked.

The party, with all the food we could eat, made quite an impression, not only on the Head State Forester but also to many of the private land owners who were hunters. Needless to say, I never lacked in hunting invitations as long as I lived in the Hagenbach area!

It seems that Germans have, October festivals, but fish festivals, historical festivals, 100-year Birthday City, town, and village festivals, and numerous others. They are a celebrating group of people. Even the great Fasching or Carnival, aligning itself with our great Mardi Gras celebrations in New Orleans and in Brazil, emanating from the Roman Catholic Church, occur, not only in the large cities but also in many towns and villages in and about Germany.

Boredom, as long as I lived in Germany and could visit the villages, was never in my vocabulary. Once the language barrier had been hurdled, the doors were open. Invitations into home, free beers or wines, and German hospitality were part of my existence.

After living in the United States for about 16 years, after my return in 1984, and visiting festivals, especially here in Hot Springs, Arkansas, I realize that the contrast of festivals in Germany to here, is extreme. Though San Diego, California tended to draw large crowds, especially to the German festivals, the Hot Springs, Arkansas vicinity cannot compare with the crowd drawing events of Germany, even in the villages.

Recently I went to a food festival, here in Hot Springs and was astounded at the sparse existence of people. Good music, great food, and great facilities are always a part of the mix, but the crowds are just not there. The high population density and the purity of national make-up must be part of the reason that even village festivals are always crowded.

Another phenomenon I have noticed in crowded village festival settings in Germany, is the fact that several thousand people, sometimes many inebriated, with one of the spouses remaining legally able to drive home, there are so few conflicts, such as fights or disputes. I heard an American once remark, "If there were this many people drinking this much wine and beer anywhere in the United States, there would definitely be conflicts!"

The Germans seem to have a resiliency, especially during festivals, to get along, be friendly, and tolerable with each other and visitors. They still sing their selective songs with vim and vigor, drinking their wine or beer incessantly during the motivating songs filled with the background of brass, drums, and accordion music. I trying to grasp the rhythmic and bouncy "Schiebe," so well named by my ex wife, that comes from the verb, schieben, that means to push in German. The polkas and waltzes, mixed in with modern songs, many American, so well adopted by the Germans.

The villages of Germany have an aroma that almost talks to you as you enter them. Each one named with its sign, usually surrounded by beautiful meadows and evergreens, glimmering from fresh rains awaiting the forthcoming winter after the fall harvest. Frosts come early in Germany, especially at higher altitudes, even in late September, leaving early morning chills, so jackets and coats are always good to have in for the evenings in October.

If one drives around the villages of the Black Forest, there are always winding Bundestrassen (main highways well maintained, as opposed by the dramatic Autobahnen), that take you over dynamic creeks and streams. Scenery, almost anywhere in Germany is merely second nature. Most dramatic, of course are the villages around the Alps. Their green is "storybook," with cows lazily grazing, beautiful meadows, scenic alpine enhancement, and farmhouses that make a poet ecstatic!

The mere warmth of just being in Germany, especially in late September and most of October are, in my opinion, the ideal time to travel in that country. Be ready to tip the scales at 10+ pounds after you return from Deutschland because the superfluous supply of wine and beer will make any gourmet or diner in second heaven.

The villages of Germany, as opposed to the larger cities provide the atmosphere of splendor that make any tourist or as I was, temporary resident, one of the most enjoyable experiences in Europe.

CHAPTER 6

The German Language Opens Doors

It is very strange that I, one who never attained an average grade in the Spanish language. I took only one-year of Spanish and my young adolescent mind could barely comprehend it under Senora Bell at Little Rock High School (not yet named Little Rock Central High). Who would ever have that I would advance to the level of spoken German at the age of 30, as I did.

To me, when in high school, a second language was merely a requirement to help me graduate. It is strange how the immature mind cannot comprehend the value of such things as other languages, mathematics, or even one's own native tongue.

After living in 4 different countries, 3 European, 1 African, my realization that another language, other than English, would open doors, provide grammatic ascension, and knowledge of my own language. The exposure to Arabic certainly put a scare into me at the age of 28, when living in Tripoli, because the teacher was so extremely autocratic. The Arabic instructor I had, with other Americans sitting in the class with me, in the fall of 1960, actually embarrassed me. His mode of instruction was very traditional and rote. I, who had very little exposure to a second language, and was poor at memorization, did not realize that the best way for, especially me, was to experience it through socialization. That is to expose myself to my immediate environment of the Libyan people if I were to progress in the language.

The process of memorization with classroom repetition was not the answer to my learning style. What I needed was the laboratory of actual exposure first, build a vocabulary and then approach the language in its formal and structured setting. The time element was not on my side. I had begun to go about it in the right manner. I got out and met people, local citizens who spoke Arabic and many, because of Libya's history, also spoke Italian, another advantageous language.

But since my time in Libya was only about 5 months, I did not have the exposure needed to build on the Arabic language, which I would love to have done. I feel that learning Arabic would have definitely been valuable to me, especially with my travel experiences.

By the time I eventually lived in Italy, I had realized the proper approach by which one learns a second language, by living in a country and having a strong desire to learn that language, then attacking it formally. However, I have seem many American, especially military, who lived as guests in a foreign country and because of their work mission, simply ignore learning the language. I have also seem certain people who do not learn the language after 3 or 4 years, but the constant exposure of more than 3 or 4 years, such as 10 or more years, provides them with a usable spoken facility of the target language.

My approach to German, after my short exposure and little success, other than a few polite expressions, in Arabic, and no wonder with only 5 months of habitat there, was quite different. I approached the language as one that I knew wanted to learn and since it was a country that I knew I had a strong desire to live in, I would learn to speak it.

Many teachers were not so lucky as I and had the privilege of being transferred after only 5 months of residence living in an outpost, so viewed by many of the military, as Libya. It was not the most sought after country in which to reside, as was France, Italy, and Germany.

When I first stepped onto the soil of Germany, I began to get involved with the language. Even most American military knew the value of being fluent in the German language and many on base programs in the 1970s were innovated in order to give Americans a facility in the language.

My first step in the formal arena was to select a "private" teacher. I did not want he traditional classroom setup with 20 students but a one-on-one instructor is what I selected in order to save embarrassment of my inability to handle rote instruction and retain phrases or expressions the teacher might throw at me. I requested a female instructor at the local Berlitz School in Kaiserslautern, a city only about 16 kilometers (10 miles) from Ramstein Airbase where I taught in the junior high school. I drove in about 2 nights a week and had an hour of instruction that was very cheap at that time, perhaps $4.50/hour, or some ridiculous fee.

The lady was attractive and I enjoyed sitting at the table across from her as we went into processes of proper pronunciation, learning sentences such as "Guten Tag, Guten Morgen, Danke Schön, und Auf Wiedersehen!" As I went from village to village, or from city to city, sightseeing, I began to acquire phrases, vocabulary, and even sentences that began to open up the door of entrance into a world that would provide proper insight into a New World. The sociological and psychological cloak that harbored a nation of people that wanted to control Europe and eventually most of the world could now be investigated with the proper tool, the native language of my host country!

During my first year or two in Germany, and after some chastising by a teacher friend of mine that I should utilize German even more, and I had only been there for a few months, I began to utilize what German words I could drag up from my menial vocabulary. Ironically, I left this gentleman in a cloud of dust, in German conversation after a year or so in the country. Actually my buddy Hank spoke a broken but effective German that was acquired from dialect speaking Germans around his Ramstein Village German friends. Hank was an avid hunter so picked up German from locals, and especially in the local Gasthäuser, or German Guest houses or what we might call taverns.

Hank's usage of German was somewhat rag tag or dialect inflected but he got his messages across. Hank was a Utah Morman and loved to deer hunt. He would help me get invitations to hunt at some of the local hunting Reviers (leased hunting areas). Once I got my hunting diploma from the local Rod and Gun Club, I was on my way. I bought a .270 Remington rifle with a fixed 4 X scope and was ready to go to the woods.

One thing I learned in the hunting school where all the laws and the German hunting customs were stressed was that before you shot anything, especially a deer, the game must be identified so that you shot the right animal. Certain deer were to be shot and one did not shoot a deer that was not designated by the farmer or person with the hunting rights of a designated hunting area.

The passion of the American hunter (military or civilian) if he or she were sincere about getting involved in hunting in Germany was well facilitated through the American military. The Status of Forces agreement set up after the end of WW II laid out a great plan that allowed American military and civilians to hunt and take advantage of hunting in Germany.

Many opportunities to practice intercultural events were through the hunting privileges set up through the military and the Rod and Gun clubs throughout Germany. There were "Stamttische" (these are usually tables in taverns or "Bierstuben" where familiar persons get together) and parties set up through the Rod and Gun clubs to promote cultural exchange. The hunters, if avid enough to pursue the hunter's diploma in Germany was usually one who would make the effort to learn the German language.

If one did not take advantage of the culture he or she would be out in left field in Germany. The language was the key to inroads into the minds of the Germans, hunters, hikers, fisher persons, bikers, "Volksmarches," or other active participants in the German events. There were always numerous activities for inroads into learning the German language.

Even the foot soldier had opportunities to meet Germans. The Germans were not shy and probably more aggressive about seeking out Americans at every given opportunity than the Americans were at invading German activities.

The door of opportunity really opened after I finished my Berlitz private German lessons and eventually enrolled into university level courses and began to study German in its formal setting with beginning courses at the extension of the University of Maryland. Most of their instructors were German Gymnasium teachers or the highest level of high school. They were excellent in grammar and usually well read in German authors and almost always had a Latin background and were great in knowing the proper German conjugation of verbs.

After several courses at the university level, the doors even opened wider because I began to attack the language in a methodical manner, with proper verb usage and a better acquisition of vocabulary.

My wife, Brigitte, was not a scholar in written German but, as many weak writers do, she mastered the techniques in speaking the best form of high-German, perhaps shy of university level and enriched vocabulary. But my German professor who also taught with me at Ramstein Junior High, commented about my wife's spoken German because it was dialect free.

I have been told that Hanover and north of it, one found the German High German to be more prevalent and somewhat dialect free. Actually my wife, after leaving East Prussia in front of the charging Russians toward the end of WW II, spent most of her childhood years around Kiel. There is a dialect in that area too but fortunately my ex wife enhanced by a concerned mother, learned high spoken German in its truest fashion.

Socially, my blonde, ex wife, was a charmer around social groups and spoke German in a rapidity that put most local Germans on guard. She had a marvelous spoken command of German that I learned to speak, almost as rapidly as she could. Actually, for pronunciation, and correctly spoken German, she was the best home teacher anyone could have.

It was later in my years of living in German that I began to speak German in a fashion that other Germans really had difficulty in identifying my speech mode. I was often asked, "What country do you come from?" Many of the Germans I met would take a guess, and many would ask, "Are you Dutch?" This was actually a compliment because most Americans who learn German often have difficulty in speaking German in a manner where they can hide "r" in its American harsher sound as they try to blend it into German conversation. The German "r" is somewhat trilled and the tongue is placed on the roof of the mouth, giving the proper intonation.

Dealing in the language and being around a German family of my wife, was a laboratory that certainly enhanced my spoken German ability. Actually it was such a proficient practicing laboratory because of the passion involved in German family interaction. The passion I developed in my ex wife's family was intense because it involved various family decisions, many Christmas or Easter dinners, and family coffee meetings.

The coffee time is so customary in German that it not only gives one a chance to add to the waistline but also the opportunity to get into passionate discussions about everything from politics to sex. The variety of beautiful and tasty cakes, rum based, lemon, fruits, chocolate, or almost any desired sinful and beautiful sweets can be found in many German homes and especially the famous Konditoreis (confectioner shops). These are absolutely a dream for those who love long leisure like afternoon moments of conversation and enjoyment.

One can spend at least an hour and maybe longer drinking coffee or tea and enjoying the sins of these delightful confectioner shops. One think, if a man, "Oh, these are not for me, one so masculine and a lover of hunting, fishing, skiing, or other outdoor sports." Wrong! These places turn women, men, girls, and the most sports loving of males on!

On some Saturdays and Sundays many of the most elegant of Konditoreis are often so crowded one has to wait to be seated, especially in the afternoon from 2:00 p.m. until 5:00 p.m. They are centers of family meetings, rendezvous, and simply great places for relaxation.

The Konditoreis are often places that provide a place for chatting, Germans and foreigners a haven for summer, spring, and fall relaxation. The winter snow, rain, or wind can motivate one to quickly escape into the warmth and elegance of the elegant confectioner shops of Germany.

In larger cities such as Munich, Hamburg, Frankfurt, and even Wiesbaden, often have music for Sunday afternoon dancing. The beautiful fox trots, waltzes, and even soft swing dancing are often the mode. Some of the confectioner shops, especially those connected to SPA hotels extend out onto the balconies and provide full orchestras for Sunday afternoon enjoyment. I found that my American visitors or relatives who made their first trip to Germany were often elated to enjoy the environment of such pleasant and tasteful Konditereis. These Konditereis are actually coffee and cake type locations. A Kafee might be without Konditerei, meaning there are no cakes served in them. The Konditerei has the coffee and cakes.

These Konditereis are also an excellent place to exercise the use of the Germany language. Many a Saturday afternoon have been sauntered away, lazily, and with conversation, either with my family, or with people whom I met in these lovely establishments of charm and beauty.

The Germans are great conversationalists and really enjoy trying out their English if they have a facility in it. After developing a proficiency in German, I seldom spoke English unless someone was curious to hear my accent and discuss my region of dwelling in the United States.

It was not until about 1970 that I ventured to change my field of study and discovered that my facility in the German language was above average for an American. After having 12 semester hours in German, spoken and written, at the University of Maryland, I discovered, through a conversation test administered by the military for CIA (Central Intelligence Agency) recruits, that my German was quite good. Since I was 40 years of age and about to get restless with teaching that I ventured to submit an application to work for the agency. The tester told me my test that they administered ran off the top and it was the highest he had ever seen.

That certainly boosted my confidence in spoken German. My facility for written German is not nearly as good as my conversation and after hammering out my syntax, proper verb usage, and pronunciation. I had my wife, a built-in conversation coach and I realized that my love for conversation and contact with the German people really paid off. The CIA test turned out to be an exercise in futility, other than proving myself on the German conversation exam, because I was rejected with that agency because I was married to a German and this was enough to disqualify me from the new job.

I am not sure, to this day, why I would have wanted to join the CIA except for an opportunity to utilize my German language. Teaching with the Overseas Dependent Schools was an adventure in itself and gave me the opportunity to travel and even live in other countries.

Most of my intense conversation in German came through some of the many contacts I had with my wife's family and also the German hunters.

There was Onkel (uncle) Walter and Tante (aunt) Else, my mother-in-law, and all the brothers and sisters of my wife, Brigitte. She and I had similar backgrounds, family wise, because she had 8 in her family, 4 sisters and 3 brothers, and I had 9 in my family, with 5 brothers and 3 sisters. There were always relatives to visit during Christmas, Easter, and even our Thanksgiving vacation because of my school schedule. The American military schools abroad had, of course, the same vacations we had in the United States.

The opportunities to visit and converse with Germans was unending. The intensity and passion of the many conversations set me up for a laboratory that is unachievable in an institution for a German major. And even with the proficient vocabulary and all the practice, I must admit, the adjective endings in German still present a challenge. The formality I had in studying German, in my earlier years kept me somewhat acute, but even today, as time as widened between the days of formal study, the language can still be difficult for perfect and expertise in its utilization, especially in writing.

My speed at speaking German is as fast as my ability to converse in English and my ex wife was the model to follow. She often spoke with the rapidity of a machine gun, as many Germans often pronounced. She was passionate, verbose in conversation, and strong in opinions.

It is quite amazing that conversation in German did open doors for me, not only in Germany but also in other countries. I was often mistaken for a German since my wife was with me when traveling to other countries or living in other countries. Even Americans we ran into in many European countries thought I was not American. While living in Italy and beginning to speak that language after a few months, American tourists would hear me switch from German to Italian, then to English when confronting them.

I truly believe that if I had majored in languages, such as French and German, at an earlier age, it would have paid off because I do like to verbalize so would venture into other languages, whether it was Italian, German, Dutch, and even some Arabic when living in Libya.

To this day I believe that the motivating factors in a foreign language are the "desire" or attitude and actually living in the country. If one does not have the proper attitude and has a built in resistance, then one can remain in a country for years and not learn the target language. This is especially true if one has the home country, as many U. S. military and civilians abroad had, then he or she can remain a long time without learning the language. I find this to be quite abhorrent, especially if one shuns the language or tries to wield English as "the" language of the world. I realize that English is one of the leading languages of the world but those who speak it as their mother tongue should not disrespect other languages and cultures.

Utilization of a language when one is a guest in that country is, in my opinion, almost a necessity, merely as a matter of respect. Even if one does not speak it fluently, then one should try, as I did in Libya. I went to classes and at least learned some phrases, though the language was quite difficult. Today, if I lived in an Arabic speaking country, I would delve into the conversation without fear. However, when I first arrived in Libya, I was very slow at picking up the language, though I tried, thereby showing a good attitude toward the language.

I shall never forget, when I first arrived in Libya and was swimming on a beach of the beautiful Mediterranean Sea, I ran into a French soldier, about my age, and he and I tried to converse with each other. He spoke his native tongue, French, and I being a newcomer abroad, spoke only my native tongue, English. We tried to hammer out a conversation. I recall, that he, trying to be polite and wanting to get to know a young American teacher, asked me, "Sprechen Sie deutsch?" Meaning, do you speak German? "No," I had to reply, "I only speak English, but hope to someday learn another language."

The conversation was short lived and I knew that my goal in my overseas career would be to learn another language someday. There were many encounters such as that one where my facility with only English kept doors closed.

My point, for any person going abroad or to even Mexico or Quebec, is to at least learn the niceties and show the proper attitude. I was very proud to wield my knowledge of German, as a teacher and as an administrator in the Dependent Schools. I received a lot of respect from building personnel, custodians, local German engineers, with whom I often worked, and the German-American structure in, especially, the German communities where our schools were located.

My positions, as an Education Program Manager, one of the titles I has at Bad Kreuznach American High School and as a building principal in Kitzingen, Germany, brought me in contact with many German citizens. We had engineers, transportation personnel, and liaison persons who did extensive work with the American forces. To be able to easily converse in German raised my status and I certainly received the respect of the military and the German civilian personnel so heavily involved in building programs and transportation services.

I also got enough insight into the German people to understand their attitudes and values. I have written about my interpretation of the future German behavior as we move toward a solid world setting with transportation and communications bringing us closer together. But this topic is one that can be explored in my book <u>The People Hitler Left Behind.</u> The Germans are a very proud and literate population. They will have to be dealt with, politically, in the international scene, with an acknowledgment of their existence in order to utilize their potential strength as they move toward a leading force in Europe.

Their almost arrogant attitude, because of their somewhat structured school system, will certainly keep them in the forefront technologically and scientifically for many years to come. This is only a hint of what my insight is into their psychic.

The inner circles of my many hunting friends and their families led me into some interesting insights into deep conversation, from past war experiences (WW II) to their economic and social structure in Europe. Many of my hunting friends were teachers, lawyers, doctors, engineers, and businesspersons. The intricate dealings because of tight and meaningful friendships were a wealth of exploration for utilization of the German language. Even some of my hunting friends who studied English did not have the facility of English that I had in German, and I was propelled into realms of understanding that are difficult to achieve because of the almost twenty years of living, hunting, socializing, and exploring in Germany.

When I say exploring, this would mean delving into the psychological minds of the German people. I love the German women, their beautiful allegiance toward family and the home, and the German male, quite respectful toward ladies and the family.

The hunting community of Germany is an almost elite group because only about 8-10% or so do delve in the sport so it leaves it as a somewhat of an elite sport. One must have extensive schooling, proper training in shooting, game identification, knowledge of seasons, proper insurance, and knowledge of the customs and ceremonies that are an integral part of hunting.

This, again, will be explored in a later chapter (chapter 12) so I do not want to delve into this extremely important part of my past experience abroad. Most of my hunting was done in Germany, with an occasional hunt in France.

This hobby, however, elevated my opportunity for conversation and interrelationships in Germany to a level rarely achieved, I would wager to say, by Americans.

I often think of some of the attitudes expressed by Ernest Hemingway, especially in his book, Across the River and Into the Woods. I was infatuated by the book and his knowledge of hunting around the northern part of Italy. That is close to Pordenone, the area where I lived for one year while teaching at Aviano High School. I do not recall the details of the character in the book but was impressed by the subject and his play of character and why Hemingway loved hunting, as I also do.

Many of the social events involved in hunting were many passionate events, with many meals after the hunt. The pleasures of fellowship, wonderful meals, great Mosel and Rhine wines, beer drinking, awaiting future invitations, and hoping that on the hunt that day, you left a proper impression on either the State administrator or Forester, or on the person leasing the hunting area, if a private hunt.

One of the special persons I remember, and who invited me to many pheasant hunts west of the Rhine, near Karlsruhe, Germany, was Henry Hatterscheid, now deceased, but retired from New York, as a waiter. His family estate remained in Germany and was carried on by his family but he returned to Germany after saving money from his retirement as a waiter in New York City. He had about 500 acres of land and a nice home west of my home in Hagenbach, Germany, near the Rhine River.

Henry never had a hunt, usually with 5 or 6 hunters, without making a fantastic meal for all his shooters. We would shoot the European Hare, the partridge, and pheasant on hunts not far from his farmhouse. Henry loved to hunt, farm and eat. He would always serve pheasant, hare, or partridge dinners. His wife was a superb cook and was traditional in her Rheinland-Pfalz manners. Wine or beer was always served with the most magnificent meals one could imagine.

I would bring him a bottle of vodka or whiskey from the military liquor store, called the Class VI store. If he wanted a turkey or something special, I would get it at the commissary. He always insisted on paying for it in pheasant. When a hunter hunts in Germany, he must purchase the game from the farmer or land overseer. This seems quite in contrast to what the Americans are accustomed to but it was fine with me as long as I brought home game and I always did. The pheasant only cost about seventy-five cents a bird and the deer was sold by the kilogram.

These elaborate hunts with meals afterwards were fabulous in that they allowed the exchange of conversation in the German language. Henry spoke English, with an accent but I always spoke with his wife and him in English. They were about the most gracious hosts I have ever encountered. American citizens but they still maintained their German traditions.

Other hunts allowed conversation during the drive hunts and some elaborate feeds after the hunt, especially pheasant, hare, and any deer that might be in the drive. Some hunts were large and there were sometimes as many as fifty hunters, always many of the hunters with well trained short and long hair German dogs.

The wealthier land owners with large spreads of 800 to 1,500 acres would bring out big kettles of bean soup, goulash soup, and great bread and cold cuts with plenty of wine and beer. The Americans, military or civilian, would love these hunts because they were in such great contrast to what one does in the United States.

Of course most hunters cherished the idea of having to at least try to speak in German. One thing I did learn about the American civilians and military was that if they were passionate enough about hunting and getting the license, they would be passionate in trying to learn to converse in German.

All in all, it must be said that when one lives in Germany, if he or she does not learn German conversation, the many doors that could be opened via the native language were closed.

The bright and invigorating experiences one received from knowing the language, especially a country as exciting, beautiful, and wonderful as Germany, were vast. The intensity of communication with the natives of Germany so accelerate the levels of understanding that one is propelled into an immense sea of endearing and rich experiences, that could not be matched by many others on the road through life. Not only for Germany but any country when one is residing or visiting, learning communication skills in the target language is a must in order to really know the culture!

CHAPTER 7

U. S. Military and Civilian Advantages Abroad

The military existence in Western Europe and especially in Germany provides unusual opportunities and advantages while living abroad. Not only does one usually have a tax free living allowance when working for the Department of Defense or being in the military.

One can usually calculate about a 30% saving in food and alcohol. The percentage of savings in gasoline for travel could be about 65%. Not only does one receive the benefits but there is the opportunity to travel, via vehicle, and see the many cities, towns, and small villages in various places as I did in Europe, with a more restricted travel radius where I lived in North Africa.

My first experience driving in Tripoli, Libya, a city with a population of about 551,000 inhabitants (1982 figures). The country of Libya in 1982 had only about 3.2 million people. The people when I lived in Tripoli, 1960-61 were obviously very poor, but the landscape and the desert, along with the beautiful Mediterranean did provide interesting scenery and exploration of the caves and seeing how very poor people survived, even in caves and huts proved to be eye opening.

There were existing Roman ruins to the east and west of Tripoli so they provided an insight into old Roman settlement. It was not unusual to wander around the ancient ruins of Sabratha and Leptis Magna and actually observe how ancient Romans lived.

Other than exploring these scenes, there was little to do other than eat in some of the restaurants of Tripoli and perhaps a few coffee bars. The hotels and restaurants, some Italian and Libyan restaurants with the Mediterranean foods were quite nice.

My stay in Libya was cut short by the unexpected transfer up to Germany, one of my target countries of my schematic plan to eventually get to one of the prime countries where Department of Defense teachers could teach-Germany, Italy, France, or Spain. France, other than American private schools is no longer an option of teachers with the Department of Defense Dependent Schools.

My exuberance regarding my designs for living in one of these countries was unerring when I was a young man of 28 and I found was most excited when I discovered I would be transfer to Ramstein, Germany in about December 1960. During the last part of January 1961 I was on my way to Wiesbaden, Germany, with a stop in Marseilles, France was exciting. The DC-4 reciprocating engines (engines with propellers) had a delay because of a faulty compass and it was a good reason for the pilots to fly into the airport in this lovely city.

I and the high profile Military Dependent School dignitaries, with whom I was flying, selected a medium class hotel after we took a taxi from the airport in Marseilles. We all, including the pilots and flight crew, enjoyed a great French meal, wonderful red wine, with a great continental breakfast the next morning and were soon on our way to Wiesbaden.

As the DC-4 came through the cloud cover on this late snowy January day in 1961, I was crouching in my seat. The Overseas Dependent School

Director's wife, Sue Mason, asked me how I was doing and I told her that until I could see the ground, I was always rather tense when flying. She told me that she always kicked back, drank some red wine on most of her flights and was always relaxed. In the future, and with my twenty plus flights back and forth to the United States from Germany, Italy, and the Netherlands, I also learned the same trick.

Living on Ramstein Airbase gave me privileges I never dreamed of. After landing in Wiesbaden in January 1961, I thought I had died and gone to heaven, especially with the base privileges I received as a civilian. The guards, German and American, manning the gates were always polite and I had a couple of PXs and Commissaries from which to choose. I also had a couple of Rod and Gun Clubs to frequent, and frequent, I did. I met all my buddies from the junior high where I taught, almost every afternoon. Looking at the selection of guns for my future hunting with the Germans was one of my favorite pastimes after school. School ended at about 3:00 p.m. each day.

My buddies, Jim Cahill, Vernon King, Ray Brown, and Hank Weeks, were all great friends. They loved either fishing or hunting. Hank Weeks was the number one hunter of the time and spoke a broken German that got him into many great hunting Reviers (hunting areas).

When I think about those days living in Ramstein, Germany, my heart grows warm. The days as a bachelor, making love to my housekeeper, young, 22, and I 28 years of age, some of the teachers, males, not even making contact with some of the beautiful women in the area, I really become ecstatic. The German women, at that time, were always willing to meet a nice American male.

I would buy a bottle of German wine, probably a 2 liter bottle from Rheinland-Pfalz or the Mosel, or the Rhine area, and put it in the window so it would get cool enough to drink in the evening with cold cuts or snacks

I bought from the commissary. What a life I had! Before I met my German wife, I was carefree and drove from village to village, seeking enjoyment, enlightenment, or new adventures.

Each morning I would go into the Officer's Club and have my breakfast, read the Stars and Stripes to see what was happening in the world. Later I could explore the Cuban Missile Crisis, the Berlin Wall crisis, or events happening during the Cold War. Kennedy was President of the United States in those years and one never knew what was going to happen in the world of turmoil. The Germans really looked up to Kennedy!

Regardless of the world events, my world was around Ramstein, Germany from January 1961 until I transferred to Italy in August 1966. I loved every minute that I traveled around Germany. First in my old standard gear grinding shift Volkswagen, about a 1956 model; it had gears that were not synchronized, so I would grind the gears, tearing through the forests between Ramstein Ari Base and Ramstein Village. What a life.

Drinking beer and eating superb food at Lili's Restaurant within only a few kilometers from my BOQ (Bachelor Officer's Quarters) on base. Hank Weeks, my teaching buddy, Mormon, and great hunter, married, with one child, adopted from Germans, and his lovely Mormon wife, always ready at home with a meal, even if Hank came home late from drinking pop top beer in a German Gasthaus. (tavern).

What days of youth, if one wants to call the age of 28-30 youth? Never a thought about what was going on back home, only what was going on in the new Germany. The separation of West Germany and East Germany was, of course, a pain in the thought processes of the Americans who now, militarily, had a hand in the control of German defenses against a probably threat from the East, the Soviets. But with the pilots around such bases as Ramstein, Sembach, Rhein-Main, and other bases in Germany, there was not much worry. The word "Scramble," was an innate part of the American

Air Force's vocabulary. The young pilots, often seen drinking in the various officer clubs of Germany, on most military bases, were living it up and stressing the meaning of the word "Scramble," meaning getting the jets up and at em in case of an emergency or an attack from the Soviet Union!

We, as teachers, gave little credence to such boasting by the American pilots and thought all of the "Gung Ho," though they, the pilots, took it quite seriously.

We survived those years, 1960-1989, though, with the safety bosom of Daddy U.S.A. protecting us and giving us the security we needed to survive in taking care of the military's children in the various schools.

We loved it. Chasing the teachers in the schools, marrying them, bedding them down, proposing to them, dating them, chasing German women, and loving the security of the advantages of the military programs abroad!

The warmth of Germany, then, as now, I am sure, was superb. I loved the quaint restaurants, and especially how far the American dollar would go in that era. About 25 cents would buy you a large beer and maybe 50 cents would buy you a great glass of white or red wine. Of course the Germans were noted for their white wines, but do not ever, ever, sell their red wines short! I had some great experiences with the German red wines, especially around upper Bavaria, in a town called Kitzingen, some of the most fabulous experiences I had, as a principal in a small K-3 elementary school belonging to the Department of Defense Dependent Schools near Wuerzburg, Germany.

I absolutely loved the food, wine, and people of that area. I could write a book about just aspect of my life when I returned from the United States on my one year sabbatical leave to enhance my administration units and my German units at San Diego State University from June 1983-August 1984. What an experience, with wonderful living and a wonderful experience with a great landlord in the town of Kitzingen, in the Upper Bavarian State of Germany

My God, what a life I had in Germany! Could it be real? Those years abroad, and the highlight of rich living in Germany. The U. S. Military provided me with experiences I could never afford from my own pocketbook, even if I had earned millions from industry or the corporate world in the United States! The experiences were unending. "Wake up, Larry, was it real?" Yes it was and I must have been the envy many people, especially teachers in the 1960s and the 1970s! A live to be envied, I am sure.

The rich and vigorous life I enjoyed from 1961 until 1984 was, with out a doubt, ineffable, and I loved every day, every minute of my vigorous contact with the German people.

Rod and Gun Clubs, PXs, commissaries, and reduced rates, were they real? Indeed they were. What a live, and all were paid for by the Department of Defense of the United States of America. The unending possibilities to travel where I wished in Europe in the 1960-1980s was an opportunity one could enjoy, only under the cloak of such an organization as the United State s Department of Defense! It was wonderful, and I, as well as all those other teachers participating, so well deserved all the benefits provide them during those years.

Teachers certainly did their part and those where were military also contributed what was needed to be a part of our overseas operations. Our years of toil and contributions to our nation by sacrificing our time abroad were exciting and certainly helped the mission of the military abroad.

My years in Germany were exciting and profitable in the intercultural exchange I enjoyed during those years. I learned the language and enhanced my target language of German by continuous contact with my wife and the German people.

Some of the other hidden benefits of living abroad were the uses of dental and medical facilities. Although I must admit that a good medical plan such as I had in San Diego, California, was more convenient than dealing with the military. Although the dentists and doctors on the bases where I lived were excellent and the services sufficed, I found the good medical plan in San Diego, along with the optical insurance, to be of excellent quality.

Fortunately I met, socially, many dentists, doctors, and optometrists while living abroad. The military will take care of you when living in the overseas environment. Their first mission, of course, is the care of the troops and families but my wife and I received very good treatment and my wife endured a hysterectomy while I lived in Bad Kreuznach in about 1979 and she was well taken care of in the Frankfurt Army Hospital.

I underwent all my dental services as well as she, my wife of that time. We received considerate and good quality treatment. When I became a school administrator, it seemed they even had a keener consideration than when I was a teacher. Educators with the Department of Defense Dependent Schools seemed to have a high degree of respect among the dentists and doctors, or at least in my experiences of being served by them. Several dentists and doctors were guests of my wife and me, and respected my bilingual ability, especially, since my German was quite good.

I heard many teachers complain at different times but I consider the facilities and support of the military to be good plus and would give them a B grade in most cases. Teachers who do decide to pursue teaching abroad can rest at ease in anticipation of their dental and medical care with military medical personnel. I would not hesitate, as a young educator to go abroad and put myself in the hands of the military.

The advantages of working with the military has innumerable advantages because of the tremendous opportunity of learning the host languages and travel that working within the United States does not compare, in my opinion.

The old adage of "I haven't even seen all of my own country," is, I believe, complete hogwash. The richness of having a home abroad and one that is constantly being evaluated and seemingly improved by military and civilian personnel who work with the Department of Defense is well worth the experience.

Even on a visit, from Germany, to Italy and Spain proved to be experiences providing unending protective facilitation by the military. There were duty stations in Spain and Italy that proved to be supportive for my wife and me.

Once, on a visit to Spain, my wife got a sudden toothache and we stopped in a U. S. Air Force base for treatment. It was near Zaragoza and my wife got the initial process of a root canal that she completed on her return to Karlsruhe, Germany, after our spring vacation trip down there. On a trip to Rome, we were provided with the best available prices in approved hotels by base travel services. The base support services for dependents is continually making agreements with hotels in various countries to completely care for and provide discounts to military and civilian personnel of the American military.

Hotels, for the everyday traveling European, even in the 1960s through the 1980s, were still somewhat expensive, but American military and civilians were provided discounts by merely showing U. S. military identification cards. I found that this card was sometimes more valuable than a U. S. passport.

Not only were good discounts provided through base services but the convenience of military BOQs (Bachelor Officer Quarters) or NCO (Non-Commissioned Officers) quarters were usually available, and one always there would be warm, clean and comfortable rooms. I found this as somewhat a double security while living abroad. Nor was the U. S. Embassy available in various countries, in case of emergencies, but the U. S. Military Bases were at our disposal.

How could a young teacher, if one chooses this profession, not choose teaching abroad over teaching domestically. There is, in my opinion, no comparison, merely because of the richness of living abroad. The military personnel of the United States still roam the earth in large numbers, and the trend now is seemingly a move away from the heart of Europe, although the NATO missions might provide various opportunities in the future. It is therefore an advantage for young teachers who want to explore the opportunities of some of the newly admitted NATO countries.

Although I consider such languages as Italian, German, and French, to be the more usable languages, I see not harm in picking up such languages as Czech, Hungarian, or even, and especially Arabic. Also the opportunities for countries such as Korea, Japan, and now perhaps cultural exchange programs such as China, would, in my opinion be exciting and adventurous. But I would always recommend the double security (Embassy plus U. S. military) by working through the U. S. military.

My early experiences in Germany, of jumping into my Volkswagen, filling up an extra gasoline can and heading for the hinterlands of Germany, are almost erasable from my memory. The richness of enhanced existence during the ages of 28 until I was well over 50 years of age could not, in my opinion, be matched within the interior of the United States.

There is no boredom while living abroad. It was, for me, like living a 25-year full paid vacation, with security provided by the U. S. Military. They gave me the satisfaction, support, education through travel, and logistical support to make my 25 years richer than the average school teacher living in the Continental United States, could ever have.

Even the clothing I purchased abroad, numerous tailored suits through the PX services of the various bases that supported me, such as; Ramstein Air Base, Brunssum, the Netherlands, Aviano, Italy, Karlsruhe, Germany, Kitzingen, Germany, and Tripoli, Libya, was high quality. Upon leaving Germany in October 1984, I left about 45 tailored suits in the hands of a second hand clothing shop in Kitzingen, Germany, hoping the nice German lady would send me a check. Since I was returning to San Diego, California, who would expect a check. No doubt she sold the high quality suits and I was relieved of excessive baggage. I never received the check and often wrote it off because of the tremendous cultural experiences granted me by my job abroad and the German people.

Not only did American teachers abroad, which worked for the Department of Defense, have the advantages of shopping in the PXs or commissaries but they also had the opportunity of shopping in local economy stores. These were for both food and clothing, of the local economies and I utilized foreign clothes and shoes during my tour abroad. When I return today I often buy needed shoes or clothes on the local economy in Germany. I like, especially their shoes, since many German men tend to have a wide foot such as I have.

The quality of the German clothes seems to be quite good and I have worn many suits, overcoats, socks, and shoes produced by the Germans. I shopped at both places, the military PXs and local economy. I loved going into the German food stores, often highly specialized, such as fish markets, small grocery stores, and even super centers. They are all glorious to walk about in and enjoy the various fresh, good quality products.

What can one expect if he or she is a young teacher and going to Germany, for instance, in the everyday work at a school on a military base? One can expect to follow the rules of the military, such as safe driving, very slow on bases, sometimes no more than 20 kilometers/hour (about

12 miles/hour). Always show identification cards on entering the bases, be expected to receive considerable help from manned military on entering the bases, if you have the identification cards, and be able to utilize the shopping and eating facilities

When one lives in outpost areas, as a civilian teacher, say in Turkey, or when I was in Tripoli, Libya, in 1960-61, there are usually military flights of morale. Example: In 1960, during our winter holidays, all the teachers on base were flown to Rome, Italy the day after the last working day of school ended, and then flown back to Tripoli a couple of days before the holidays ended. These were morale flights and I find them to be absolutely superb for American teachers living abroad. Once the teachers landed, I am sure they headed to many locations in the heart of Europe. What could be more exciting?

Actually I missed that flight because of not getting the word about provided travel orders but made it up by rushing to Civilian Personnel and having my orders typed out and getting on a hop flying to England and then on to Evereaux, France. Made no difference to me. The military broke their butts getting me on a flight to get out of Libya for about 15 days during the winter vacations. I was flown out on the airfield at Wheelus Air Base in Tripoli, Libya, and jumped onto the warming up, taxiing transport, jumped on and asked where they were headed? "We are headed to England, then to France!" "That is fine with me, I shouted back to the crew member!"

These are just some of the excellent and loving concern that military showed for me while living abroad. There is a special concern of the troops for teachers. Maybe it is a respect they developed in high school. I tended to get into very few conflicts with the military. Perhaps once I got into a dispute, the only one I remember, over not leashing my Dachshund dog I was walking around the military officer housing in Ramstein. But this did not get out of hand, but evolved with a little sarcasm on the part of me and the major with whom I was doing battle. We resolved our differences once he realized he could not pull rank on me and I realized I should follow the rules, so leashed my dog, Suzy.

Another way the military facilitates the U. S. military is by providing university level educational programs. All of my German courses up to my sabbatical in 1983 were taken through the University of Maryland at Ramstein Air Base and at Vogelweh near Kaiserslautern, Germany, a U. S. Army base. They provided excellent German teachers with the University of Maryland and I got my first 12 semester hours of spoken and written German from excellent grammarians. The German accent with a great facility of proper grammar in the native language was right there, only a few minutes drive from my base housing and about 2 nights per week.

Later, I taught for the German Volkshochschule (German adult education program) in Bad Kreuznach, Germany. I taught conversation English to various adults who wanted desperately to learn English. The Volkshochschule loved having me, especially since I was Assistant Principal at Bad Kreuznach American High School and I maintained substantial numbers in my evening classes, made good money, and had repeat students.

The numerous opportunities that one has abroad are innumerable. The only syndrome I felt myself moving into while living abroad was that I had become somewhat "Germanized" if there is such a word. At one point in my life, I became so closely associated with the Germans, speaking the language, joining in the cultural events, hunting with them, and socializing with them, that I began to feel as closely with many Germans as I did with my own American friends.

I developed a deep and intensive closeness with the German people. But I do not see this as a fault and many people, who remain five or more years in a country, and develop a working knowledge of any language, may begin to feel the same closeness.

But the U. S. Army or Air Force was always there, providing my pay, sending me home on leaves, and providing me excellent support, so the danger of falling into the doldrums of expatriate existence was hardly a problem in the long run. Also, there is an innate immunity with most Americans living abroad. We are so well indoctrinated into patriotism, I do not feel that the expatriate syndrome is really a problem for people who live on extended assignments abroad. Many military personnel, especially those married to Germans, received multiple tours abroad. The Vietnam War did, however, tend to break up some of those tours, unless a G.I. was in a field where the German missions were critical to keeping them there. One of my hunting buddies was married to a German woman and spent over twenty years in Germany, and most of it near Bad Kreuznach. His specific field was communications and he knew a lot about the wire services, telecommunications valuable to the base services.

Many military service personnel, who married German women and had families, usually with children who were bilingual, thrived on the prolonged military assignments where they remained in Germany tour after tour. After all, the wife was happy and the children had become accustomed to either going to a military dependent school or to the local German school.

There were many afternoons after I got off work from the high school in Bad Kreuznach that I would go out to the woods with my buddy who worked in communications, then hunt until dark. My buddy's name was Sgt. Knottingham and I hunted with him about 4 years in the Bad Kreuznach area. He had a contact out east of Bad Kreunach who took us deer hunting and sometimes we got in a little duck hunting.

If I wanted anything in the area of communications, such as an extra telephone instrument in my private home, he could help me out. If I needed any extra extensions in my office at the school he would fix me up. These contacts are what made my living around a military base worthwhile.

Living in Bad Kreuznach was extraordinary anyway because of my wife's great relations with the community base commander who was a full colonel and this, in turn, led to a great contact with the commanding general who was with the 8th Infantry Division. My wife and I were made official receptionists at such functions as Christmas parties, Thanksgiving events, and community balls. We were made official interpreters for people entering the officer's club in that area.

I really enjoyed the inroads that my wife, a miss personality plus, helped me with. She was charming when it came to dealing with the military. She had a private interest because she was a German realtor with the full license and had a side job of helping the troops get into rental houses on the economy. She was assertive in business and always had the best deals, would look out for any pitfalls the troops might fall into with the Germans. She knew all the ins and outs of rental contracts and could get a place for a new officer, NCO, or enlisted personnel who had a housing allowance.

Actually, my ex wife, Brigitte, made a lot of money through her pension or her rental and real estate business. She had it going in every direction but was always fair with the troops and the Germans. I have never seen such an assertive business woman in business.

She loved the interaction and her utilization of very functional English that I helped her with. I directed her toward about 2 years of university work at the University of Maryland extension. She made the Dean's List with my constant work in her history and English. She loved getting a double dose of education; what she had learned as a dental technician and what she picked up at the University of Maryland.

Brigitte was delightful, well-dressed, and top notch when it came to German American relations. She charmed the base commander and the commanding general of that area. She knew people in high places in the city political structure in Bad Kreuznach and was always ready to lend a helping hand to newly arrived U. S. military or civilian personnel coming into the area.

She was always aware of what was going on and took full advantage of the programs surrounding the military establishment. She taught German to the troops, assisted families new to the area, and became well known with the community military personnel as well as the mayor and other political personnel in the Bad Kreuznach area.

We were astounded after learning, years after I left Bad Kreuznach, that a couple of families we had both known, I through the school, and Brigitte through the community, that a couple of families were caught in a Cold War spy ring. A couple military NCOs were caught in a espionage case. Two specific military personnel were feeding information back to the Soviet Union and both were sent to prison.

There was always a lot of excitement around the military bases. The greatest thing about working for the military, as previously stated, was the low cost of living, the PXs, the commissaries, the low cost of gasoline, alcohol, and advantages in low cost touring. Any person having a chance to work with the military abroad and utilize the military privileges would be wise to take a position, expand his or her travels, and reduce his or her cost of living in such an environment!

CHAPTER 8

Golden Ghettos

One of the fascinating things about living abroad, especially on a military base is the complete, almost cradle to grave protection the military adorns its personnel with.

If a military family, sponsored by officer, NCO, or enlisted personnel, wanted to go abroad, even now, it would be completely insulated, if it wished, from the local civilian setting. The bases have all the necessary shopping, housing, restaurants, movies, and almost the things an American has back home. One can get hamburgers from the local snack shop, usually attached to the PXs, pizza, or most of the familiar fast foods found in the United States. When I fly back and observe some of the bases, though I do not have privileges, I notice such things as Burger King and some of the standard pizza type parlors attached to the bases.

Sometimes the "Golden Ghetto" syndrome must really give the security that the non-traveling and uninterested military dependents love. Many of the military families that I observed would never leave base, but just stay on the base for its somewhat secure protection. There were bowling alleys, movie theatres, various shopping facilities that would provide 100% of the things needed to isolate oneself.

I think that today, however, there are programs that promote cultural exposure, such as language, and intercultural exchanges and encourage families to get about into the villages or adjacent towns near bases.

One could stagnate in the 1960s and 1970s when I was in the highlight of my stay abroad. Unfortunately, the ones who stagnated and did not take advantage of the German, French, Spanish, or Italian culture, depending on the duty station, were usually the underpaid enlisted personnel. They sometimes chose to remain on base and live in the comfort of their protected American environment. Maybe that is fine but living abroad offers many opportunities to travel, learn another language, and get to know other cultures.

So many of the bases seemed to promote a protective environment for American personnel in these days. Today, however, I know that the status quo is for new arrivals to learn the host language, travel to learn, and simply expose themselves, whether civilian and military, to the local communities and the environment of the country one is stationed in. Or at least that was the aim in the late 1980s. But the closing of so many bases in Western Europe in the late 1980s gave way to fewer American personnel abroad. Seemingly today, and now I am continuing the writing of this book, even in 2005, most of the European troops have been redirected toward Bosnia, Afghanistan, and Iraq.

I used to wonder why the Russians didn't drop a bomb on Ramstein Airbase on a Sunday afternoon, if they wanted to really choose to attack the Americans. But I now realize that the Russians were so poor and their military was nowhere near the quality of the American military. But maybe the Russians did not have planes and weapons sophisticated enough to do such a thing.

So many of the Americans were at home in their base houses watching the military television services and trying not to lose their acquired American culture, that the Russians could really have played havoc on our military and civilian personnel during the 1960s and 1970s. Of course we too were so deeply engaged in Vietnam War that our money and focus tended to move toward that lost cause war.

My passions today, are seemingly different. I tend to be more forgiving toward the lazy G.I. who coddled his family, remained on base and let the officers drive the local highways and German autobahn to explore and learn about the invigorating and exciting new culture about him or her.

Golden Ghettoes were created to take care of the military personnel who lived abroad in the 1960s, 1970s, and 1980s. They created a home environment for Americans who did not want to expose themselves to another language and culture. That is fine, if one wishes to remain ignorant of the environment about one.

Today, it seems, in the 2000 era, the troops are flown into Iraq and remain there for a long time, sometimes dying for their country. It is sad since it all seems to be about oil.

The Golden Ghetto, however, was a place I resided in while I was stationed in Ramstein, Germany from January 1962 until August 1966. I at first lived in a BOQ or Bachelor Officer Quarter. I actually did need more room and little did I realize that the cold in Germany, especially in the villages could be drastic. I got quarters off base after I was in teaching at Ramstein Air Base for about 6 months. I wanted to get out and mingle with the Germany people and that is what I did after I moved off of base around November 1961. I rented a 1 bedroom lower part of a German family's house in a small village called Bann, near Landstuhl, Germany, not far from Ramstein Air Base. The small village is different from the West German Capital called Bonn. I loved living in Frau and Herr Kehrer's house for the first few months after I moved in the late fall of 1961.

After I got married in June of 1962, I brought my wife, Brigitte down from Kiel, Germany, after she had stayed with me a couple of months prior to our marriage in the spring of 1962. I got so tired of living alone and missed her company that I corresponded with here after she returned to Kiel to work and live with her mother. It was almost like a conspiracy because her mother knew if she left me alone, I would miss the compatibility and having a woman by my side. He mother was exactly right. I did miss her company and the constant companionship.

Brigitte and I got married at the St. Nicholaus Church in Kiel, Germany in June of 1962. I took about a week off from my work at Ramstein Junior High School and took my wife on a short honeymoon in Hamburg, Germany, a fascinating city. It was one of the cities that got bombed extensively during World War II.

We knocked around Hamburg for a couple of nights before returning to our house in Bann. I had, by the fall of 1961, a new Volkswagen, 2 door, as they were then, air cooled engine, but good on snow with its air cooled engine in the rear of the auto.

When I first got to Germany, I bought an old, probably a 1958, gear grinding Volkswagen to knock around in. I traveled to many places in this old auto that I bought from a colonel in the air force because it was a second car and I paid him about $300 cash. It was suitable and I drove it from January 1961 when I came to Ramstein from Tripoli, until the fall of 1961.

From June 1961 until August 1961, I flew back to the United States to attend Vanderbilt Peabody University and pick up credits toward a degree beyond my master's degree in sociology. I planned my own coursework and eventually dropped out of the degree program, then began picking up science and mathematics courses because they were more valuable to me in my teaching.

I also started studying German at the University of Maryland that had a degree program for the military and civilians abroad. It was convenient for me and I loved learning about German grammar and adding courses to my college courses.

I only wanted to become proficient in the German language and was achieving just that goal by the time I left Germany to transfer to Aviano Air Base that would, in 1966, become my next duty station.

CHAPTER 9

Bella Italia

The one distinctive thing I remember about living one year in Italy was that I regretted leaving the two-year assignment after only one year. My early departure from Italy would become because of a new school that would be built for NATO and I would be one of the chosen ones but that will be revealed in a later chapter of this book.

My wife, Brigitte, in August of 1966, drove two autos down from Ramstein, Germany, to my new assignment, the American High School in Aviano, Italy, not far from the beautiful Adriatic Sea.

I was to teach algebra at the ninth grade level and also had some 7th and 8th grade mathematics courses. I loved the students there since they were air force and delightful, every one of them. They were curious, intellectual, and had great parents.

The Italians were friendly; trusting to the Americans because they knew the U. S. Government was behind the troops, civilians, teachers and other personnel associated with the air base.

It was a challenge trying to learn an additional language to my already well-acquired German and Italian had a ring and friendliness to it that I could not find with Spanish. My only experience with the Spanish was my one-year in high school and a couple of visits I had had in Tijuana and one trip to Spain.

Relishing the friendliness, sunny weather, and gorgeous scenery in the rolling hills and mountains descending down from Switzerland and Austria would make my stay in Italy delightful.

It is amazing that today I speak with many Americans who have been to Italy and when I convey to them that I actually lived in the land of wine, beautiful vineyards, seashores, and mountains, they never fail to give me a positive evaluation on this gorgeous country.

My accessibility to the Adriatic Coast and my love of my 1965 Volkswagen Cabriolet (convertible) made my months there a dream. Even though I was married, my wife spent a lot of her time in the process of adopting our daughter, Liane.

Some of my friends, teachers and technical representatives with corporations supporting our military intensified the social charm about the base. The officer's club was delightful with its Mediterranean motif and an open patio that allowed in the beautiful rays of sunshine or the beauty of starry nights.

It was pleasant sitting at the bar, when my wife was visiting Germany, and listening to Frank Sinatra sing "Strangers in the Night." Every time I hear that song I am suddenly catapulted back to that setting at the officer's club at the Aviano Air Base in Italy.

Most of my fun was driving to the seashore north of Venice and relishing such towns as Carole and other small towns along the Adriatic coast. The pleasant lunches with grilled chicken, delicious white wine or Italian beer made my age of 34 even more delightful.

Gazing at the gorgeous Scandinavian, Austrian, German, French, British, and who knows what other nationalities basking in the sun with their bikinis and most certainly many without their tops when they could get away with it in the more conservative Italian setting.

Brigitte and I began to take Italian lessons immediately with one of the secretaries in our high school and spent about 4 hours a week exchanging our German for the enchanting and beautiful Italian language. Getting the enunciations and subtle meanings in the Romance language was a challenge, as it was challenging to the secretary trying to elicit subtleties of German. My wife spoke a beautiful High German and mine had reached a level of prolific conversation.

Within a couple of months I was ordering my own gasoline and food from restaurants with very little effort. Shopping also became easier, although so many Italians enjoyed switching over to German when they spotted my blonde German wife. They adored her looks, with her blonde hair and fair skin. They, were in contrast, olive complexioned, dark haired and also beautiful and charming people.

I did, however, meet some lovely fairer skinned Italians in Northern Italy where we lived and they were absolutely gorgeous. As one moves from Northern Italy and ascends into Austria, this mixing of blood between the Germanics and the Italians becomes more obvious.

Many of my weekends were spent in the Villach, Austria area. Villach is in the southwest corner of Austria and offers one the spa setting or the hot baths found in many German cities and also Austria. They are favorite places for people getting treatment for various ailments.

Villach had many good restaurants and Bob Earle, a fellow teacher of mine who taught social studies in our high school would take trips for the weekends, sometimes without his wife, and mine spending a lot of time making arrangements to adopt our child.

Bob and I enjoyed drinking beer and taking good whiskey from the Class VI Store at the air base when we would drive up to Villach, Austria. We enjoyed conversing with the Austrians, waitresses, restaurant-owners, hitting the bars, and just having a good time. The food was exceptionally good and since both of us had lived in Germany, we enjoyed the Germanic food such as Wienerschnitzel, various selections of sausages, chicken, and Bratwurst.

Bob, my fellow teacher, had a tendency to drink much more that I so he would often get a little inebriated in the late evenings so we would both end up flirting with some of the waitresses, especially the beauties of Villach so we would often have to be careful because the restaurant owners did not cater to two happy American civilians flirting with their hired help.

I, and another teacher, Earl Hansen, who was an avid skier would also either drive up with my wife and me to Villach. Sometimes we would rendezvous in the Villach area. Earl had a Yugoslavian fiancé who was a fantastic cook. She was a nurse spoke the language of, I believe what is now Bosnia so we would often extend our weekends, especially the long ones on into Yugoslavia out of Austria by heading more directly south out of Villach rather taking the southwest direction toward Aviano.

Eventually Earl Hansen married Teresa and she later passed away in the mid 1970s. I heard it from him through a letter because we continued to correspond even when I left Aviano for a different assignment.

I was always watching my budget and remember on one event when my wife and I joined Earl and Teresa, along with a technical representative of one of the supporting corporations servicing the U. S. military communication systems about the airbase in Aviano, Italy. Earl suggested that we take a Saturday drive to the mountainous area north of Pordenone, where Brigitte and I had our apartment, not far east of Aviano Air Base.

Earl said we could have a lunch of cheese, bread, and a couple bottles of wine and it would be relatively cheap. I remember that it cost each of us well over $20 or the equivalent in Italian Lira, and that was a lot of money for me at that time since it was $10/head. I thought and knew that if one was cautious, such prices could be beat by merely going into a food market and purchasing these items. It seems that Earl dragged us into some restaurant and the prices in that mountain village were sky high!

Some of our weekends were spent in Venice, which was a charming city, and it was only about an hour southeast from our apartment in Pordenone. We would drive down to the pier, hop on one of the passenger boats and then hang around the St. Marcus Square or some of the coffee shops or bars in Venice and those experiences were most charming. The city of Venice, completely surrounded by water had also been a hangout of the great writer, Ernest Hemingway therefore it proved to be an area with a lot of charm for American visitors. I believe Harry's Bar was one such place that Hemingway often visited when he visited the area.

One of the books I enjoyed that took the Northern Italy setting into Hemingway's account was, <u>Across the River and Into the Wood</u>. It was a book I read with great delight because of my treks along the rivers and valleys north of Venice.

Just sitting around the gorgeous St. Marcus Square and enjoying a glass of wine and having lunch was more than one, as an American, could expect in satisfaction as a temporary American resident residing in the region.

Some of our trips took us as south as far down as Rome and Naples. We made several trips west and southwest from Pordenone and often visited the Italian Riviera, Pisa and Florence. We, on a couple of occasions, visited Niece and Monaco to the west of us, winding around the curves that snake around the Mediterranean through numerous tunnels that lead into the French Riviera.

Rome has a charm of its own and at that time, 1966-67, the American military had an agreement to give discounted hotels that we were provided for its curious military and civilians. A list of these discounted hotels was provided from the air base, and one could get great deals for our then, somewhat limited budget. Our budgets, as teachers, were certainly limited if one made a practice of seeing any and all the tourist sites around, as long as our money held out however, we continued to make the trips.

The traveling that I did when single, then after I was married, was very extensive, even when I first located in Germany. The challenge of hitting the open road in a Volkswagen, first my old one, then the new model that I purchased in the early fall of 1961, and later the 1965 Cabriolet proved to be worth every nickel spent on transportation, just to satisfy the hunger for exploration of beautiful Germany, France, and Italy.

While we lived in Italy, we did most of our traveling in our little Volkswagen Cabriolet, white with a black top and we were exhilarated, as it would sail along the Italian Autostrada at a very appropriate speed of sometimes 70 and 80 mph. Many of the Italians, like most Europeans, tend to drive at breakneck speeds in Europe since they are not burdened with lowered speed limits.

One would often see Italian automobiles that had been speeding and would run off the highway, causing, sometimes, multiple crashes. The Italians in their Alpha Romeos and other fast vehicles were as bad as the Germans in driving the Autostradas at break-neck speeds.

It was during the Christmas holidays that Brigitte and I proceeded to return to Germany and adopt our ten-day old daughter. We did this through an adoption agency in the Hanover region of Germany.

We spent Christmas with my wife's mother and relatives, with everyone showing excitement about our newborn child. We had an exciting Christmas and soon returned to Italy so I could resume my teaching in January of 1967.

We actually smuggled our daughter through the Italian border guards but with the military license plates, there was no problem.

The faculty at the American school in Aviano gave us a nice reception and gifts for the baby in the month of January 1967. We were well liked in that school and I was instrumental in getting a teacher's organization started there so I was well respected. The teachers at the Aviano Elementary and High Schools did not seem to be aggressive with the Civilian Personnel group there so I brought, with me, some of the more assertive and legal concepts we had used in Germany for organizing a teacher front under the well known AFT (American Federation of Teacherss), associated with the AFL (American Federation of Labor).

By March, my wife had to return to Germany with the baby to complete the adoption papers. She spent almost two months in Kiel going through that arduous process before she would complete the paperwork toward the end of April.

On one occasion while my wife was going through the adoption procedure in Kiel, Germany, I took a long weekend trip, after taking Friday off from teaching, toward the northwest and into Switzerland for a rendezvous with an Austrian girlfriend whom I had met through one of the technical representatives from the air base. She was a gorgeous lady and was the receptionist at a nice hotel-pension in Locarno, a pleasant Swiss city only a few hours from the Aviano area where I resided. I drove across the northern top of Italy, enjoying the beautiful scenery before I made my way north to Locarno.

I spent Friday and Saturday night in the hotel-pension and she showed me around the area. We enjoyed dinner, lovely wine, and had a marvelous time. I had met her at the SPA City of Villach, Austria because that is where her home was. She was with her boy friend, Bob, and I enjoyed speaking German with her and enjoyed her Austrian dialect. It was charming, as was she.

At any rate, this lovely lady proceeded to give me the time I wanted with her because she took off work so showed me the mountainous area so we enjoyed breakfast, lunch, great wine, and some of the local nightclubs around Locarno and even on to the southwest at Lake Como, a place I had already frequented but did not know it as she did. She introduced me to some lovely outdoor Cafes overlooking Lake Como, so the charm of spring was in the air, presenting a beautiful setting.

We had a great lunch there and enjoyed the very beautiful spring weather. It was sad, later, through contact with my previous friends from the air base in Aviano, to learn that sometimes in the 1970s, this lovely person was killed in a high-speed auto collision. I do not recollect her name but she was a charming and a lovely person.

I returned to our apartment in Pordenone and continued my teaching the next week. It would only be a few days until Brigitte and Liane would return from completing the adoption papers in Germany.

Brigitte finally brought the beautiful baby back into Italy and we spent the beautiful spring enjoying our travels with little 5 month old Liane being carried around in a basinet and even enjoying sleeping while we dined in the finer restaurants around Aviano and Pordenone.

Around April I learned that since I had applied, sometimes in March, for a position in a new international school in the Netherlands, I was accepted for a science position in the new "concept" and 4-nation NATO School.

My principal, a Mormon and rather strict but efficient administrator had tolerated my aggressive behavior since I had many contacts with the Overseas Dependent School personnel in Karlsruhe, Germany, and really was sure of my often extreme demands for new texts and curriculum support.

At any rate, the principal came to me and asked that I not leave Aviano but remain at the high school in Aviano. He had gotten to know me and value my ability as a teacher and leader. He made the plea but I had a good contact with Dr. Joseph Mason, the director of the overseas operations so I would accept the new position since he personally selected me for the position in Brunssum, the Netherlands.

Brigitte, Liane, and I prepared for our summer leave in the United States where I would be attending a summer program under the National Science Foundation. They paid a stipend and I would be studying mathematics and physics at St. Cloud State College. Brigitte and my baby daughter, Liane would remain in Warren, Arkansas with my mother while I spent 6 weeks studying in Minnesota. I drove my mother's auto and left my daughter and wife remained in the small town of Warren, Arkansas. My mother had other transportation provided by an elderly lady my mother was looking after. It turned out to be a great summer for my family and for me also since I only had to hit the books and do some fishing in the lovely area around the lakes of Minnesota.

We returned to Milano, Italy, drove back to Pordenone and picked up our dog, Heidi who had stayed with a fourteen year old Italian girl who fell in love with our prize winning Dachel. Under the young girl's care and training, she, Heidi, won 3 medals for beauty in a Dachshund dog show that summer.

Once we took the dog away from the crying girl, we made our way back to Germany, then to Brunssum, the Netherlands, my next duty station and would soon be living in a small town called Schinveld, on the German Dutch border and in the vicinity of Aachen, Germany.

I was in for a real adventure at the new school at Brunssum, location of a closed coal mine but the old mine sites were used as part of AFCENT Headquarters under NATO. AFCENT (Allied Forces Central Europe) proved to be one of my most interesting teaching tours.

CHAPTER 10

The Netherlands and Its People

Dutch is a most difficult language and its guttural tones, attached linguistically to the German language, were difficult, not only for me but for most Americans about AFCENT.

Fortunately I had a solid background in the German language, and in the southeastern part of the Netherlands, the people were seemingly friendly toward German speaking people and my wife and I used German quite often there. English was also well liked but when I could not come up with the Dutch words, the Dutch people were kind when we tried Dutch. Both languages, German and Dutch were frequently spoken in the area.

In the temporary quarters where my family and I resided, about 6 weeks before finding permanent quarters, and in a town called Kerkrade, not far from Aachen, we found the location to be acceptable and not far from my school in Brunssum.

It was only about a 12-kilometer drive to the school in Brunssum so it was not bad. The landlady and landlord, Frau Graus and Herr Graus, were both excellent in doing special things for us and provided breakfast in their wonderful home because it was included in the rent.

They loved speaking German with us and for some reason, did not hold a terrific grudge toward Germans, so the treatment they received from the German occupiers during WW II must have been tolerable.

The Graus family also adored our darling ten-month old Liane because they simply loved having her around their lovely well kept home. It is known around the Netherlands that the living room windows are kept open for walkers by to gaze in and look at the well-kept houses.

We had a private bathroom and bedroom and could use the kitchen, dining room and living area freely during our six-week stay with the Graus family.

We got to be good friends of the Graus family and often had them visit us when we finally found our new 3 bedroom, 1 1/2 bath home in the small border town of Schinveld, only about 4 kilometers from my school AFCENT International School. Schinveld was a small village that was a stone's throw from the German border and one could actually enter the Netherlands in that small town.

I also had a great and dear friend in the neighboring German village directly over the border from Schinveld. I knew the Burgermeister of that German Village and he and I became great friends because he had hunting land (leased) right on the border of Schinveld but in Germany, for pheasant and also had about 2,000 acres of land in the Ardennes Mountains in Germany.

I spent many weekends with Herr Dr von den Driesch, a well off doctor in that border area of Germany. We would sometimes, even after my school day was finished, hunting pheasant and partridge. It was a blast because I had acquired my hunting diploma while living in Ramstein, Germany and only had to update my hunting license through the German State offices in order to hunt.

We shot the Reh or Roe Deer down in the Ardiennes Mountains and I actually shot, after leaving the Netherlands, my first wild boar on a high seat, after I was later reassigned to a high school in Karlsruhe, Germany but that would be down the road from the tour of 1967-1971 in the Netherlands.

Not only was there much fun hunting, again in Germany, but the travel throughout the Netherlands proved to be great. We got to Amsterdam, Rotterdam, The Hague, and all the small towns and villages throughout the Netherlands. What a life I had living in the Netherlands while I was 35 years of age until I was 39 years old. This was a time I was young, virile, and still enjoyed feminine pulchritude. It was often tempting to want to go astray, even though I was married and though most of the time I remained faithful to my wife until I hit my last year at Brunssum, I was difficult to keep my pants buckled.

My German wife was free with me because I would drive to Aachen on weekends, go to various bars and got to know some young German students and professional people about Aachen, getting to various bars and Cafes in Aachen.

We, still had two automobiles so I would go out on weekends, party, drink beer, and gad about the exciting city of Aachen. I stayed out of trouble with the German and Dutch ladies but the American teachers were the ones who were the most dangerous.

There must have been something about American male teachers being married to a foreigner because it seemed that most of the lady teachers I met did not care if I were married or not. They seemed to be fair game, so to speak, and they all liked to party and have a good time. I stayed in trouble!

Toward my last year at AFCENT, I had begun an affair with one of the teachers in the high school in the American section of AFCENT International School. We had 4 sections; U. S., British, Canadian, and German. I was the science department head of science in the American section but we tried to departmentalize by including all the teachers from all four sections at our department meetings and internationalize where we could; teacher exchange, etc. Some German students were allowed to take English courses from the British section or the American section, depending on the focus of their English; the English with a British accent or that with an American accent.

Then if a German student wanted to have an exposure to American History, the best place to do it was in the American section. Some of this crossover process occurred but not to a great degree. It was a trend and a focus of the administration and if one returned to the AFCENT International (NATO) School in the 1980s, I wonder how much crossover would have been accomplished?

CHAPTER 11

Karlsruhe, Germany

In 1971 I made my move to Karlsruhe, Germany, by request of my director and immediate supervisor, the principal of the American sector of AFCENT. I was being moved and given an assignment as a science teacher at Karlsruhe American High School.

I knew the director of the Dependent Schools of most of Europe and was later to become the director of DODDS (Department of Defense Dependent Schools) world wide; all the U. S. American Dependent Schools! This was exciting for Dr. Joseph Mason, whom I had known since my assignment in Tripoli, Libya at Wheelus Air Base.

I was sent to Karlsruhe to teach and I would be right under the wing of Dr. Joseph Mason, a traditional Ameriocan school person whom I had long admired. He had to vie for maintaining his leadership but had the advantage of being with the dependent schools of Europe and was now (1971) to become the director of the world's U. S. military bases.

We often had a drink together at the Karlsruhe Officer's Clüb, Smiley Barracks, right in rthe middle of Karlsruhe, Germany. This turned out to be a terrific assignment because Dr. Mason had a knack for getting his teachers assigned there if he liked them and I feel he really did like me since I met him at Wheelus Air Base, Tripoli, Libya and rode on a plush plane put together for personal flights of the then King Idris of Libya, who reigned from 24 December 1951 to 1 September 1969. His full name (reference https://en.m.wikipedia.org) was Muhammad Idris bin Muhammad al-Mahdi as-Senussi!

I flew to Wiesbaden, Germany in late January 1961 for my reassignment to Ramstein Junior High, Ramstein Air Base. I was transferred to this wonderful junior high because I was short of biology credits, which I later accumulated to complete my academic background in science, making me a more valued teacher for possible future school assignments in science.

On the way Wiesbaden, Germany, where Dr. Mason was then headquartered, we stopped in lovely Marseille, France at their airports because one of the guidance compasses went out on the plane so we all got a hotel and enjoyed a fine French dinner at one of the noted restaurants of 1961, though I have long forgotten the name. But with Dr. Mason and his wife-to-be, Sue Mason, though they were not married at that time, fine restaurants were always the accepted mode.

The next morning after the plane was repaired, we took off and headed to Wiesbaden, Germany. As one can imagine, the weather in Wiesbaden, late January turned out to be icy, snowy, and unfriendly. But we landed in that plush DC-4, military plane all plushed up for King Idris making it a comfortable and fun ride.

After spending a couple of nights at one of the military facilities, the American Arms I believe is where I spent the night before the train ride to my forthcoming Ramstein Air Base.

I arrived at the train station, Landstuhl, Germany, only a couple of kilometers from the airbase where I was to spend about five years (1961 to 1966) on a fantastic junior high teaching assignment.

Ramstein was in a fantastic location and provided me with a fantastic pivoting point to Wiesbaden, Mainz, Heidelberg, and even Baden Baden, once I

But these are reflections back to chapter four when I related my experiences of Ramstein, Germany and its junior high where I was so happy for almost five years before getting assigned to Aviano, Italy.

Dr. Mason and I had fond memories together as he did with many other educators in Europe. He was my person of advantageous contact and was, I am sure, responsible for my promotion to assistant principal at Bad Kreuznach American High School in the summer of 1977.

My overall experience with the German citizens and hunting in the beautiful reviers near Karlsuhe, Germany and along the Rhine River are experiences I shall never forget.

I built relationships with many of the German citizens who were aristocrats of the German society and to this day I still reflect back on them. I also made contact with the very few whom I had known in the Karlsruhe area from 1971 to 1977 long after that time frame.

My chapter thirteen, "The Hunters of Germany" will give me the opportunity to expand on the realms of hunting, the hunters, and nature of many of these fantastic people about Germanuy!

CHAPTER 12

The Hunters of Germany

It was at Ramstein Airbase, the fall of 1961 that I acauired my German hunting license which allowed me to hunt any game in the Bundesrepublik. My class only lasted about a month and the American military and civilians were granted, through the U. S. and German Status of Forces Agreement, to participate in German hunting classes and obtain a bonafide accepted hunting license for Germany.

I took the course and after falling through with a not so acceptable score on my first attempt, with about a dozen other candidates, we got through the course after some review. But the course for the German citizens requires l lot more study and time. I think it takes over a year and possibly longer for a German citizen to conquer the German hunting course and obtain a hunting license.

The license had to be renewed each year if I remember correctly and was obtained at one of the local German state administration offices. Or the Rod and Gun Clubs attached to the air bases or army bases provided avenues for the license as the Rod and Gun Clubs provided the hunting course for military and civilians.

The hunting in Germany is most always through invitation, either by private revier (hunting land) owners or via State facilities. The German foresters all obtain hunting licenses for their federal foresters. The concept of integrating hunting and balance of game with their food supply is an integral part of the German "Abschuss Plan" which is a scientific concept of keeping the proper food supply with the proper amount of land the game is located on.

In the hunting classes, one studies the gestation periods, the type of game indigeneous to the area and the balance of that game population to its food supply. The Americans in the United States do this to some degree but not to the extent the Germans do.

At any rate, the process is very scientific and only serious hunters attempt to acquire the German hunting license. The concept of going out into the wilds and shooting all the game you can bring down is not a concept accepted by German hunters. The German hunters and Forsters (forestry perssonel) are very serious about harvesting game.

With all their serious endeavors, the Germans do something the American hunters do not take so lightly and that is they drink during or between a morning and afternoon hunt. The Germans diligently drink alcohol, either while hunting, on what is known the "line" which may be a large field or an area in the woods where the hunters are lined up with probably twenty to thirty meters between each hunter. On this line, one of the persons helping the land owner will come by and serve schnapps, a strong clear alcohol beverage! Americans are much more discrete about such matters and consider drinking, in most cases, to be a dangerousmatter when it comes to mixing alcohol and shooting firearms.

Also, there are usually, especially during a private landowner hunt, various and plentiful foods served with wine, schnapps, beer or gluhwine (a hot wine (red or white) mixed with sugar, for warming oneself on a below zero temperature day. The hunters of Germany think nothing about alcohol being mixed with shooting pheasant, the hare (large rabbit of the field, weighing, sometimes as much as twelve pounds or five to six kilograms}, deer, or even wild boar.

Also, there are various types of hunts, either in the fields or wooded areas that are dog driven, "the drive hunt," or sitting in a high seat waiting for a deer or wild boar to come to a feeder below, or just wander out of the wooded area below or near the high seat. Some hunts are merely walsing, slowly, through the fields or woods, usually with a dog, waiting for the game to be driven out by the dog, or the hunter, quietly comes upon the sought animal.

Also, when hunting in Germany, the hunter is expected to dress properly and that is with a green or brownish colored jacket, knee pants, or long pants, that blend in with the green forests of the dull colored fields, depending on thee time of the year. A hat is to be worn at all times during the hunt. It is usually a brimmed hat and somewhat sylish and they are usually of good quality. While the American hunter usually wears the cap type with a camouflaged color, but also often brimmed, the Germans usually have a more stylish brimmed hat, sometimes with the bristles of a shot wild boar or feather of a pheasant or some semblance of bagged game attached to the hat!

The hunters of Germany are, compared to the American hunter, made up of a small percentage of the population. It is very restrictive, as stated previously, to have the previlege of hunting in Germany, whereas, the American hunter traditionally has had very little formal training, until the most recent years of huting in the United States. Many states have in the last few years, probably late seventies and eighties, innovated some training or short game and fish commission classes which tend to mimick what the Germans have been doing for years, and that is training or schooling hunters.

My knowledge of the hunting in Germany comes from twenty years of experience hunting with private estates and well defined state controlled hunting areas, mostly in the Rheinland-Pfalz state of Germany, with muchof the hunting being done in the vicinity of the Rhine River, which runs very close to the village or "Dorf," of Hagenbach, Germany. Many of my wild boar hunts were done just a few kilometers, bordering the country of France.

I also had the good fortune to do a couple of state hunts in the vicinity of Munich, Germany, while studying with Florida State University extension, in about 1971. I booked a hunt through the state agency near Munich and went on a deer hunt (the Reh deer, usually about thirty-five U.S. pounds, but was not successful. The State Forrester who accompanied me was diligent and obliging but we were not succesful. The hunt was a few kilometers from the city of Munich in the direction of Chiemsee but I do not remember the specific location. Anyway it was a beautifuly summer day and an afternoon hunt. We left the woods late in the evening with no game!

I was fortunate to hunt pheasant along the Rhine River, near Speyer, Germany, where we saw hundreds of pheasant on the land of a pleasant farmer and on his private Revier. There were about fifty hunters on that beautiful fall day and several hunts after that, all successful! Dogs were being carefully walked and controlled by their owners and the gunfire, after the hunt started was quite plentiful, with hundreds of pheasant spiralling upward from being jumped by the aggressive short hair, and other types of fantastic German hunting dogs! It was a sight to behold and lies firmly in my memory bank today....this being over fifty years ago!

Other hunts have takein me to France, the Ardiennes Mountains, where the Battle of the Bulge was fought during the tail end of WW II! I was fortunate enough to have been invited to that area and shot my second wild boar from a "high seat" or "Hochsitz," so called by the German hunters. This outing led me to shoot my second wild boar, about sixty kilograms (about one-hundred and twenty-pounds) at about 2 a.m. on a snowy night in December. The hunting area was a private Revier owned by a doctor friend of mine whom I met while living in the Netherlands and who was the mayor across the border from my home town (Schinveld, the Netherlands). This doctor was mayor in the town of Gangelt, Germany and was a sincere person who invited me, quite often to hunt on his land, whether he was present or not. Such privilege is not so often acquired by hunters in the scheme of things, while hunting in Germany!

The only hunt I had outside of Germany was near Metz, France, whild I lived in Karlsruhe, Germany. The base commander was a colonel, Gilbert Poitiers, a colonel in the French army. He was in charge of several hundred Hectare (a Hectard is about 2.2 acres by U. S. standards) and invited about thirty hunters to hunt wild boar, on a drive hunt. Several were shot that day but I was not one of the fortunate hunters. This particular, later to become a general in the French army, was my brother-in-law and I had spent, with my then wife, Brigitte Stell, many weekends visiting, as he has spent many weekends visiting me in Germany! We were and are still very good friends. He had two lovely children, now grown thought the son died of cancer in the early 90s I believe.

The hunt in France was successful for some of the French hunters and they were avid hunters and seemingly well trained, as are the German hunters but I am not familiar with their hunting methods and processes.

And as far as my one tear stay in Italy, I did not get to join up with the local Rod and Gun Club at the Aviano Air Base, near where I was stationed 1966-1967. I had the guns and clothing but never got time to check out the Italian hunting processes.

The only thing I did not write much about was my collection of guns and it was rather small compared to the German hunters I knew, with about nine guns in my office in my three-thousand square foot, second floor, apartment and part of an old beautiful home only a stone's throw to the Nahe River, Bad Kreuznach, Germany. My guns, rifles and over-under shotguns were all assembled on wall gun racks, openly in my office.

When I returned to the United States in 1984, I sold all my guns to my other, German brother-in-law for a plentiful sum of almost ten-thousand dollars and he did, I assume, the proper paperwork to transfer those guns from my military records to the German documentations needed. Neverless, he is now deceased and I assume the guns were either sold of handed down to his sons.

So the overall scheme of hunting in Germany, as I, an American citizen, view it, is a process of proper education and training about the age old hunting processes in Germany. They have a beautiful traditon of enjoying the hunting in their country and even up to the 1980s there was ample game in Germany.

Today, 2016, as I am now continuing to write this book, I presume the balance between game and forest/fields, is still plentiful, although with the creeping of city expansion throughout Gemany, now a country composed of the defunct Eastern Germany and Western Germany is one country and I presume tnhe hunting traditions are still beautiful and bountiful for all the hunters of beautiful Germany!

CHAPTER 13

The Educators of Germany

My experience with German educators was probably more extensive than most American educators, in that I belonged to an informal group of school administrators while working as assistant principalof Bad Kreuznach Americah High School, Bad Kreuznach, Germany during the time frame of 1977-1982.

I was also fortunate enough to have been selected as a teacher of ESL, English as a Second Language teacher in the German evening Volkshochschule. This was an evening class for Germans who wanted to learn English but were tilted toward learning from me, as their English teacher, the idiomatic English. Idiomatic English is a process which provides the learner to delve into a certain English usage, privy only to someone who has been brought in the setting providing one with kowledge of terms such as, "Let's get on with it!" or "He was in hog heaven!" or "Put a damper on it!" So many terms that the formal foreign student never picks up while under the teaching processes of the instructor. Only a native speaking teacher of American English can impart such nuances to the learner.

I also had many students who were business people of Bad Kreuznach, come to my classes and would take my course in sequence; beginning to intermediate, then on to advanced classes. I also had some of the sixteen to eighteen year old Gymnasium students (Gynasium is the most advanced high school system of Germany). My evening classes were even more satisfying to me than my daily routine as a secondary school administrator who deals with everything from discipline to dealing with the school budget.

But one of the most enlightening think about being a local school administrator was when my princpal, the person above me, or my boss, did not want to partake in local pedagogical intermingling, such as the local Bad Kreuznach and area of school administrators, both secondary and elementary meetings or socials. These events were assigned to me because my German was acute and more advanced than my bosses, previous or existing! So I took the assignments and had a wonderful time communicating, gossiping, talking about common problems or just enjoying each other.

I, being a very social person and enjoying people, was very successful at such events. Actually there was a conservative and a liberal local mayor (Bügermeister). I happened to have gotten along with Herr Schindowski versus Herr Schmidt, at that time, about 1978-79) who was the liberal SPD mayor and we were very good friends, throwing accolades to each other throughout our frequent conversations over a glass of wine or dinner, somewhere in the heart of Bad Kreuznach, enjoying a dinner, usually supported by the mayor's office, as far as costs go.

So these adventures, gathering of local school administrators lasted as long as I was still employed by the U. S. Departmentof Defense, usually in the form of an expensive dinner or luncheon at some local Bad Kreuznach restaurant, and usually one of the finer ones. These events continued, with Herr Schindowski usually footing the bill with the city's finances. We even went to wine tasting at the local wine school, "Wein Schule" in the heart of Bad Kreuznach.

Once or twice we ventured into France, near the border of Germany and enjoyed the wine tasting of France in the not too far distance from our German border and spent several nights touring the wine areas of a close by French wine growing area. This event, much to the chagrin of Herr Schmidt, the conservative (CDU) mayor got wind of the event and was highly antagonized, according to my then German wife, Brigitte, who knew all the gossip of the elegant ladies of Bad Kreunach. He had a tirade, so I hear, about Herr Schindowski taking a bus load of local school administrators on such an expensive wine tour that lasted about three days!

These were some of the rewards I received as the official local American school administrator in charge of school administrators social group! All these experiences, I would venture to say are were not so often experienced by educators in the military-civilian communities throughout the European militray command, though I do know, due to past employment is such places as Brunssum, the Netherlands, at AFCENT (American Forces Central Europe} such events were frequent with the higher command!

The dealings with the secondary administrators, usually Gymnasium directors, sometimes elementary directors, brought me in contact with the concepts and philosphy of the German school adminstrators. They were not, beliee it or not as reserved in their setting, sometimes, as were the Americans. For instance, it was not unusual to see a bottle of bourbon or fine scotch in the bottom of a director's desk in even an elementary school. Once I was visiting an elementary German elementary school south of Ramstein, and this was in the 1960s, and the director had me in his office and offered me a drink of black label Johnny Walker scotch, and this was mid-afternoon.

In many of the secondary German schools, after I became an accepted member of the local "CLUB" so to speak, they would speak freely about school problems, school personnel and often even about their private lives. I felt very accepted because they actually did not know whether my position as assistantt principal was equal to their highest positions as director or what my position was, compared to theirs. All they knew was that I was the appointed one for the social group of administrators and I was somebody of high rank!

This was, for me, a psychological element which elevated my ego in the highest sense. While my boss, the principal, was back in school, dealing with events that might make him for future assignments, I was enjoying most prestigious moments, being looked up on as an accepted member of a social group, most of them highly recognized in the community of Bad Kreuznach, and reveling in these positive moments in the highest sense.

Actually, this activity propelled me to a confident existence of self confidence I had never known before in the realm of my education experiences. Though the events and interaction was purely actions between me and my German educator colleagues, the were most prestigious for me personally.

Interesting as I look back on such events and then return to the DULL (comparatively speaking) existence in the classroom setting into which I was thrown after 1984, teaching in the San Diego area of California, the contrast of respect, intermingling with high level educators of the German community, then to be placed back into the classroom was MAJOR DULL for me and my ego!

I cannot say enough about the comparison of my life as a school administrator in the American school setting in Germany to that of going back into the classroom in the California setting, although my teaching experience of twenty-years was respected enough by the San Deigo Unified Schools to honor me monetarily in placing me at the highest level of pay because of my twenty years teaching! But the psychological blows were almost overpowering and actually the pay almost surplanted the EGO damage of not again being placed in an administrative position. And all this was because I had not built up the contact and political basis I had in the overseas setting with the Department of Defense Dependent Schools abroad!

And again, if I compare the high prestige of dealing and working with high level German administrators, the eventual pay I received from 1989 to 2001 in the San Diego Unified Schools ALMOST compensated for the EGO damage I received from spiralling back down to the level of a classroom teacher, although my several assignments as department chairperson in the San Diego schools certainly helped my EGO because department chairperson prestige almost compesated for the lost position of overseas school administrator setting.

Since I began to receive my retirement from overseas teaching with the DOD (Department of Defense) on top of my San Diego salary and I started receiving the retirement in about 1994, when I turned sixty-two years of age, my salary zoomed to almost $90,000/year.

One year I claimed about $130,000 because of a lucky gambling I hit at the Viejas Casino, east of San Diego on Highway 8. I learned to play video poker from a previous lady friend from San Diego so events like this certainly boosted my fractured id (caused by the return to the classroom).

I finally realized that had I have remained in a California school system such as San Diego Unified School District, from 1960, when I shipped out to the overseas schools, to Tripoli, Libya, I would have reaped a retirement at least twice what I would have harvested from the DOD (Department of Defense).

Since the monetary harm has been done, I feel that my experiences with the overseas setting and my spiritual gains as a previous teacher and school administrator, especially those with this particular group of educators around Bad Kreuznach, Germany, has propelled me to levels of achievement hardly attained by many retired educators.

The prestige and satisfaction of my association with the German educators of Germany so enlightened and elevated my life experiences, that I can only say THANKS TO THE FANTASTIC EDUCATORS OF GERMANY!

CHAPTER 14

The German Mind

The German mind is not to be grasped by a two week vacation in Germany or a summer stay in this fantastic country! One really has to enjoy and experience the German people over a long period of time. I would say ten years might do it but eighteen years of exposure to the German culture and German language should be sufficient time to reap the benefits of the German people, culture, language, their temperment, their likes and dislikes, and even the individual mind which can be extrapolated to the possibility of the individual being transposed into the massive mind of many citizens who are today enduring many political exposures that could propel Germany into the most dynamic force in Europe!

Eighteen years of close exposure with citizens, my wife's relatives, business dealings via my position as a teacher and school administrator because of our school needs for various facilities. Many of our contracts for building, purchases, and repairs were purchased from the Germans. When serving as assistant principal, many contracts were negotiated with German firms and my ability to speak German fluently, led to many contacts with engineers, contracting firm presidents, and German workers of all sorts.

But the most intense and intimated contact, other than hunting in the fields and woods with a high class of German citizenry, was my exposure to my wife's mother, father, sisters and her inlaws! These relatives were located in Mannheim, Kiel, Rendsburg, Bremerhaven, and Metz, France. My brother-in-law, before mentioned regarding out hunt on the French military compound, Metz, France lived, first when I met him, near Paris, France, then later in Metz, France. Fortunately he chose to speak German with me because his knowledge of German, though with a French accent kept us in a friendly and familian mode of great, warm, and cordial contact. Though he was a colonel in the French army and pushing for general, which he later became, our relationship was almost like real brothers. I did many favors for him and his family in that I purchased him merchandise (cigarettes, alcohol, turkeys, and all sorts of food from our commisaries, whether in Ramstein, Karlsruhe, or Brunssum, the Netherlands) over the many years I knew him, and that started in 1962, shortly after I married Brigitte because her older sister, Edith, was his wife.

Gilbert, whom I still respect and honor, and who is still living and also lives in Metz, France, where he chose to retire. In fact, I last spoke with him on the phone in August or September of 2014, when I last visited Bad Kreuznach, Germany.

So these intimate contaces, especially Brigitte's brothers, sisters, her mother, father, uncles, aunts, were like my own family. The German association with my inlaws was as intimate or perhaps more intimate because of the close associations with most of them was congenial; usually conversations and meals involving either schnapps, beer, or wonderful glasses of wine, white and red!

My Uncle Walter, the uncle to Brigitte, and brother of her mother, was so intimate, that we even took trips together, usually in the vicinity of Kiel, northern Germany, or even Denmark, and especially the Netherlands, where I spent my five years working with AFCENT (a strategical part of NATO), which was located and housed, partially in an old coal mine, Brunssum, the Netherlands.

Uncle Walter and I knocked around the border towns of Germany edging right up to the Dutch border and one in particular was Aachen, a city with today's population (2016) over 240,000 citizens. So the city had plenty of good bars and restaurants at the time were frequeting it and gorgeous German ladies to converse with.

Running around with my virile uncle, drinking beer, schnapps, wine, and eathing in fine restaurants, as well as partaking in beautiful German meals prepared by my lovely wife, Brigitte, was in keeping with my desire and active participation with the German element which enhanced my knowledge of the German language and culture!

The Dutch language, I must admit, was a very difficult one but one I did not actively pursue, as I had the Italian language when living in Italy in 1966-1967. I felt, though learning the niceties of the Dutch language were necessary for me as a visitor in that country, the language was not as valuable as the German language proved to be! The Dutch language was very difficult in that it did not seem to carry the prestige German carried in my travels throughout Europe. I learned to understand Dutch and speak a limited amount of the language but that was about the extent of my pursuit and I did not pursue it formally as I did the German!

So my dealings, especially with the German population, lead me down a road of high level exposure into business connections, most levels of education, intermingling withn hunters, family contact, and a multiplicity of interaction into the social realm of German society. My German speaking and much reading and sufficient, {at that time) writing the language was sufficient for an American working as a teacher for the U. S. Department of Defense and living in the country.

These experiences propelled me into interactions with the German population so that I could readily grasp the thinking processes of a most progressive set of people in the European society. The German people and their mindset as well as their, what I saw as regimented ways and varying temperments, sometimes depending on the region from whiich them came, were a people I learned to admire and respect. Much of this adminiratrion came from the observations that the whole society had vigorously dug themselves out of the ruins of an almost destroyed nation resulting from the second World War!

To rebuild and elevate a country, especially West Germany, after the occupation by allied forces, was a challenge and certainly a virtue of high motivation and high technological capability for a society!

When I first arrived in Wiesbaden, Germany, my FIRST entry into the country, January 1961, the country was still accepting U. S. money, eaual to about four plus D.M. (Deutsche Mark) to one U. S. Dollar! By the time I left the country in 1982-83, the German Mark had elevated to well over twice its value. Now, of course (2016) the Germans have conveted to the European Market Euro.

But my eighteen years dealing with many levels of German society; social, economic, educational, familial, and the realms, especially travel throughout the country, exposed me to the fantastic German mind. Why and how Germany, during the 1930s fell into the captivating clutches of a leader such as Adolf Hitler, can be well assessed and documented by history, books, studies, records, and noted actions!

I was told once by a German lady, and my evening class teacher of German, that she felt the education system of the German people could be one of the major reasons the Germans fell under the spell of their **Füher** and leader during their economical crisis prior to World War II, was that the German people, in their school system bestow authority upon their teachers and autocratic leadership and education teaches that one if to follow and obey the leadership and authority throughout the school system!

I, as a longtime observer, would give much credence to that concept that the German mind is overwhelmed with the concept of the leader, teacher, business director, military leader, or whomever the person in charge may be, one should diligently, to succeed and do the right thing for advancement and sucess, will adhere to the commands and directions of the said leader!

This concept, as compared to the functions and actions in American society, with democratic principles, whereby, sometimes we impose out thoughts and creativity into out ecucationsl, business, or professional actions and do not always blindly follow the professor, leader, or boss in our everyday setting. In otherwise, the thoughts of Americans may be, WHO GIVES A SHIT WHAT THE BOSS SAYS, I WILL DO IT MY WAY!

Even with the past military actions, in WW II or WW I, i.e. Sergeant York when he capatured all those German solders, so vividly shown in the movie with Gary Cooper, "Sergeant York," displayed the creative American mind overwhelming the regimented mind of hundreds of soldiers surrendering to a long American soldier!

The processes of a regimented mind, as I believe occur in German society, and what I have observed, can lead to the progressive advancement of a nation, especially such as Germany, advancing to a state of harmonious production and high level technological progress. These people undoubtedly produce great tenological items such as automobiles, aircraft, and multiple mechanical devices and machinery throughout their society!

So my analysis and respect for the German mind is, I believe that they are a great and progressive society, always seeking improvement and advancement to exceed above other people and countries! My personal dealings with this society for eighteen plus years led me to believe the German people will continue to succed and be on the cutting edge of society in the European setting for years to come!

CHAPTER 15

A School Administrator's Advantage

Spending twenty-five years in Europe and some time in North Africa, led me to realize that, especially in Germany, one had a distinct advantage. The German mentality has a built in direction that shows respect for teachers and educatiors!

Education is highly respected in Germany, by its people and also teachers have a respect that I thought seemed to be as elevated as doctors are in American society. There were many times I observed salespersons, professional personnel, and people in social settings regarding me, a teacher in the local American high school, treating me with a very high level of respect I never received in my own U. S. setting! Teachers were very highly respected in German society; this observation I have made many times.

It was a very satisfying feeling to have such respect in Germany. I was never reluctant to explain, when asked by many Germans I met socially, that I was a high school teacher because of the very positive praise I received.

And being a school administrator certainly brought on the accolades in various social settings, whether it was a private party or a school to school setting, i.e. German school vs. American school. "You are a school director, a "Schulrector?" was the question I received with awe when communicating with the German citizenry.

Bad Kreuznach, Germany is a city of well over 55,000 people or was at the time I lived living in Bad Kreuznach from 1977 until 1983. This a city with a lovely setting, surrounded by mountains with the Nahe River flowing gently through, on its way to the Rhine River. There were, and still are many hotels and restaurants in such a middle sized town.

Actually the functioning of the Eighth Infantry Division contributed to the exciting setting of this "SPA" city with its lovely Spa hotel only a few meters from the Nahe River. Not far away were vineyards and lovely farms with many small villages settled near Bad Kreuznach and Bad Münster am Stein, its sister city, only a few kilometers from beautiful Bad Kreuznach.

The restaurants in both cities are so inviting, with their beautiful assortment of white wines grown locally to enhance meals of wild boar, Wienerschnitzel, fish, and various assortments of German meals! I knew many of the restaurant and hotel owners and my wife, at that time, Brigitte Stell knew so many more people than I did because of her work as a realtor and teacher of German for the military of the Eighth Infantry Division of the Americna forces.

As a school adninistrator and assistant director, as I was referred to, I had an advantage of high respect bestowed on the many other German school administrators in the vicinity. The local German citizens did not delineate when I entered a restaurant of wine locale. I was highly respected and often met with locals, sometimes on a Sunday morning, to drink beer or a glass of Riesling white wine along the Spa vincity of Bad Kreuznach.

There were festivals of various sorts, whether in downtown Bad Kreuznach or near my lovely home only a few meters from the Nahe River. I lived in the upstairs, second floor, with an ample 3,200 square feet of area, a large apartment for me, my wife, Brigitte, and my lovely daughter Liane. We could often walk outside our apartment and run into a festival being held along the beautiful Nahe River. Or I could walk my wonderful, beautiful and faithful dog, Rusty, a long hair Dachshund who was the third of the three Dachshund dogs I and my wife had owned. The two previously owned beautiful dogs were miniature long haired dogs and Rusty was supposed to be a miniature long hair but when that dog grew up, it seems that somewhow the lovely creature was NOT a miniature because of his very distinctive large features. He was way above the size specifications we had previously found in our petite and lovely Dachshunds!

But dogs, especially if they are as beautiful as ours were, are highly respected and loved by the German people. Sometimes I often thought the Germans gave their attention to well groomed and attractive dogs more lovingly than they did to children!

As a school administrator and educator, walking this creature of beauty and grace such as Rusty had, led me to many conversationss, especially to beautiful German women who often pranced and strutted, well dressed, along the Nahe River in the Kur Gebiet (Spa Ares) of Bad Kreuznach.

I met many people while leading this beautiful creature along the grass covered areas along the lovely Nahe River. I met all sorts of German citizens, gorgeous ladies, professionals, vacationers, and spa guests casually ambling along the Kur Gebiet! My dog, Rusty was just a source of conversation, leading to many satisfying interactions of social interaction with all sorts of viaitors from, not only various locations in Germany but many Auslanders (people from other countries, ranging from the Netherlands to Sweden, Denmark and areas such as Czechslovakia, Italy, France, Hungary or many other countries in Europe and even the Middle East! Bad Kreuznach, for an American educator, was a small paradise!

Bad Kreuznach, because of its, not only local educators and many prestigious citizens was a plethora of doctors, business people, educators and sophisticated retires. Because of its strategic location and many clinics appealing to "well off" retired people in all spectrums past professional backgrounds, Bad Kreuznach, a town not too large and not too small, appealed to so many past successful professionals, who would not love living in this "Small Baden Baden" as one of my teaching colleagues often referred this paradise near the Rhine River with its strategic location. Bad Kreuznach in near Mainz, Frankfury, Wiesbaden, and not too far from Heidelberg, and to the northwest, Cologne and Bonn which was, before the fall of the Berlin Wall, the capital city of West Germany!

So living in the heart of Germany with a great professional status and a lovable family plus my wonderful dog Rusty, made me realize being who I was at that time, made my life satisfying as a school adminstrator!

In the summer of 2014 I returned to Bad Kreuznach, Germany to visit and stay the two months with my ex-wife and my daughter, Liane and her then husband, Thomas. Whenever I return to Germany, especially Bad Kreuznach, it is always refreshing seeing the wein locals and visit the vineyards as well. The beautiful white weins, especially the Riesling Wines are joyful, tasty, and refreshiing, so I spent many evenings partakiing in this activity with my ex-wife, my son-in-law, and my daughter.

Strangely enough, my contact with the local administrators and teachers in and about Bad Kreuznach had, of course diminished. But the wonderful Lina Hilger Gymnasium, where my daughter attended through the "Mittlere Reife" level, about the tenth grade, was still quite visible as I would walk by it or drive in my ex-wife's Mercedes. And the two mayors whom I had cherished knowing during my years in Bad Kreuznach, 1977-1982, were no longer on the scene. My classy existence as the Assistant Principal of Bad Kreuznach American High School was no longer part of my being and enjoyment.

The city of now about 49,000 is as beautiful as ever and the lovely river, the Nahe, still flows through the city and makes its quiet, now, until the spring floods emerge, with the beautiful setting of the bridge houses making this lovely city even more beautiful and quaint! Almost everyday I would frequent a coffee house enjoy the beauty of this quaint city. Then in the evenings I and my ex-wife or other friends of the past would partake in a wonderful German meal and red or white wine.

The memories still remain and persist as I walk the streets reminiscing about days of the past. In the fall, a more strategic time to visit most any German city, the beer and wine festivals begin. And in Bad Kreuznach, it is most favorable to visit in early fall when the fair or "Jahrmarkt" brings hundreds of citizens to town for bratwurst, beer, wine, and many other sorts of German foods to its guests! This coming year, 2016, I hope to take another trek to my second home in beautiful Germany and visit for a month, renewing old memories and seeing never forgotten friends!

My memories as one of the school administrators in Bad Kreuznach, Germany will live on in my memories with only positive thoughts still penetrating my brain! Germany and its quaintness and beautiful for this American educator are dramatic, beautiful, romantic, and most positive! "Ich liebe Deutschland, und werde niemals vergessen!" "I love Germany and will never forget it!"

# CHAPTER 16

Reflections of Highlights Abroad

What were some of the most interesting aspects of my eighteen years living in Germany? So many people who visit Germany reflect back on the German autobahn and its speed limits for anyone driving the German autobahns. While I was living there in the 1970s and 1980s, the German advocated a speed limit of about one-hundred-twenty Kilometers/hour. This was a speed advocated for safety, although if I remember, one could drive far above this speed.

In 1962, my brother, Jim, bought a brand new, blue XKE Jaguar convertible and brought it to my, then rented economy house in a little town near Landstuhl, Germany, not too far from my duty station, Ramstein Air Base, where I taught at the Ramstein Junior High. The town was Bann, Germany.

He decided to leave the automobile with me and have it shipped back to Calirornia after I kept the beautiful automobile for July, August, and Septmeber so the auto would be shipped back to California as a second hand auto and it saved him a considerable abount of money on taxes which were levied on new autos coming from overseas.

I had the previlige of driving this very expensive auto at that time all over my local area of Ramstein, Heidelberg, Karlsruhe, and later the auto was taken to Bremerhaven, the port from which I shipped it back to San Pedro, California. My brother, then employed by Convair Aircraft in San Diego, trusted me to keep care of the car and ship it readily back home, which I did.

I had the pleasure of driving the auto for three months as if it were my own, all around the Ramstein Air Base, with heads lifted and Americans, as well as Germans looking at this most elegant vehicle, the sports car of the 1960s, the XKE Jaguar!

One day I drove the beautiful blue auto, top down, to Saarbruecken, Germany, south of Ramstein Air Base and a coal mining town with several bars and nice restaurants. I stopped to go into a coffee place, called a "Konditerei" where coffee and cake were served, along with any alcoholic beverages, if one so desired. At that time, my salary, in about 1962, was so great relative to the income of the average German worker, I was looked upon as a rather well off person. When I returned to my brother's vehicle, the beautiful XKE Jaguar, there were about eighty people gauking and gasping at this unusual and miagnificent automobile! I, of course felt like a celebrity, and was, in the eyes of the Germany people in 1962!

I made my way through the gathered crowd, spotted two of the most beautiful ladies, about twenty-one to twenty-four years of age and gestured that both of them jump into this magnificent automobile. Both readily accepted! I, speaking some broken German, asked them where they lived and they explained they lived in a neighborhood near the outskirts of Saarbruecken. I drove them home after stopping for a drink in a bar near where I picked up the two lovely creatures! I, to this day, do not remember just what ensued ith the most beautiful Geman ladies but they readily accepted my offer to escort them to the bar, and then home.

Since I was married and had a lovely wife, I saw no reason to pursue the two lovely ladies. My wife, very tolerant and not chastising me for my encounter only laughed at the matter and lauded me for captivating town lovely German ladies who were awestricken at such a gorgeous automobile!

I also drove the automobile to Kiel, my wife's hometown to show the vehicle off to Brigitte's family. Driving on the way to Kiel, with my wife in the vehicle, I got in a race with a very nice Mercedes, one of the more expensive models at that time. I kept on his tail and I reached the incredible speed of !35 miles per hour, the fastest I have ever driven on the German Autobahn! This was a breakneck speed and thank God I stayed on the road and maintained that trememdous speed for only about five minutes!

After settling down to a reasonalbe rate of speed, about one-hundred and tewnty miles per hour, crusing speed for the rest of the trip, I brought the magnificent automobile to Kiel, where my wife, Brigitte's mother lived and visited her brothers, sisters, and mother for about five days. This was most likely Thanksgiving holiday. The journey from Ramstein Air Base was about a six hour trip.

These are the events highlighted as wonderful times in beautiful Germany. Driving an elegant automobile that was so rare, and probalby the only one in Germany at that time, about 1952, was a highlight of my stay as a young teacher in Ramstein, Germany.

Interesting enough, I had a brother-in-law, Otto Stöben, one of the biggest realtors in northern Germany and has a beautiful home outside of Kiel and owned jumping horses for a hobby. He was a generous, rich, and cultivated person, still living in the Kiel, Germany area, and whom I respect because of his great business ability and accomplishments in the real estate setting in northern Germany. He was most gracious and treated me with much respect, knowing I was a teacher. We had wonderful times together.

In fact, he had one of the powerful Mercedes of the 1960s and challenged me to a short race out to his home on the outskirts of Kiel, giving the Mercedes so much acceleration, I could barely keep up with him in my brother's XKE jaguar.

We had much fun, drinking coffee, cognac, and eating wonderful meals around Kiel, Germany. It was wonderful being among the elite of Northern Germany because of this wonderful man. He even arranged a hunt for the large European Hare, almost thirteen pounds, one snowy December day, north of Kiel. I had been hunting in the Ramstein vicinity and Otto arranged the hunt through one of his connections and it proved to be a great outing.

Wherever I went in Germany, I was always treated kindly mostly because I was a teacher with the American schools, in Ramstein, Karlsruhe, Bad Kreuznach, and later, Kitsingen, Germany, where I served for a short time as a sschool administrator.

These were just some of the highlights that strike my mind when thinking and reflecting the many years in Germany. From the time I set foot on German soil, knowing this was my next duty station after leaving Tripoli, Libya, I only experienced mostly positive experiences in this wonderful country!

Another penetrating experience happened in Tripoli, Libya when I asked a young teacher who was married and she was not really eligible for service with the U. S. Airforce because she was married and somehow evaded admitting she had a husband. She was a teacher from New York and a lovely person. On a lovely Ocober weekend, I asked her to join me for a picnic and she consented. We started our trek by driving north from Tripoli, driving my brand new white Volkswagen Beetle back through the low mountains, then drove back south toward the Mediterranean in the direction of one of the ancient Roman ruins along the sea.

But on the way we tried to stop for a drink and a snack but as we got out of our automobile and started to break out some wine and some of our food, we were confronted by men and women who emerged from caves in the low mountains south of Tripoli! The beggars would not leave us alone. We could not eat in peace because many of these drastically poor people living in caves were drastically impetuous and had their hands out for money!

We ended up visting, I believe, one of the ruins, west of Tripoli, Sabratha and walking ist narrow streets, at last finding some solitude from beggars, finally eating our picnic lunch, drinking some white wine and chatting about how fantastic it was living in North Africa and enjoying this old Roman ruin.

This is just another reflection I have in the myriads of memories and experiences of living abroad!

Other events would be the many experiences I had, driving another Volkswagen but this time about a 1965 convertible I bought in Mainz, Germany before I got my assignment to Aviano High School, Aviano, Italy. My wife and I had a gorgeous apartment only about twenty minutes drive from my school where I taught mathematics and science at the high school on Aviano Airbase, Aviano.

Our apartment was in a city west of Aviano, and the population of this lovely city today (2016) is about 50,000 inhabitants. It is strategically located near the Adriatic Sea, to the east of this lovely Italian city and only about an hour drive from the lovely city of Venice, Itally.

But most dramatically my drives were over to the small coastal towns along the Adriatic where one could enjoy the restaurants with roast chicken, beautiful wines of Italy and feast one's eyes on the beautiful women from Scandanavia, Germany, Austria and other countries north of Italy.

The drive, less than an hour from my apartment gave me wonderfuly weekends during the mild fall months and later in the spring of the year. The contrast to my many years living in Germany was fantastic just to enjoy the sunshine of this wonderful country. The mild climate was absolutely a dream and having the beautiful Volkswagen convertible made it even much more palatible!

My German wife, Brigitte was spending much of her time taking the train back to Germany and pursuing the legal adoption of our several months old baby, Liane! We had brought Liane back to Italy, although illegaly through the Italian border without problems but in essence we smuggled her through the border. Nevertheless we pursued the legal adoption of this, then a few months old and succeeded. Brigitte acquired the correct papers to make her adoption legal. We got the child at the age of about ten days old while driving back to Germany during the Christmas holidays of 1966.

So these are the highlights of my fantastic time in Italy. Along with this were my frequent visits to a nice resort and spa city of Villach, Austria, only a couple of hours drive from Pordonone, Italy. Villach proved to be interesting because it provided me with the flavor of Germanic culture which I missed, although I loved all the things about Italy!

Another highlight of that stay was the memory of my dear friend, Earl Hanson, who was a fantastic skiier and also a hang-glide pilot, belonging to the Aviano HANG GLIDE CLUB. I saw him take off a two to three thousand mountain outside of Aviano, Italy and sail down the mountain side like a bird! How thrilling it was watching this fellow teacher, skilled both in skiing and hang-gliding!

These wer some of the highlights of living abroad from 1960 to about 1983 and the indellible imprints in my mind will never leave.

As a spin-off from my many years living in, mostly Europe and a short time in North Africa, I can only advise the youth of the United States and any other country, who have the degree or credentials to teach, or work in a professional field, to take advantage of opportunities which might bring them into a profession or career abroad. Exploring the world via a good profesion and having the advantage of seeing the world in a setting abroad can only bring enhanced experiences for learning about other cultures and languages other than the immediate culture one was brought up with!

CHAPTER 17

My Return Visits Abroad

After returning to the United States in 1983, I resumed my work as an educator in the San Diego Unified School District, after studying at San Diego State University while on sabbatical during the year 1982-83. After trying a wonderful assignment as a principal in a primary school with the Department of Defense, 1983, for only a couple of months and then falling in love with a beautiful San Diego woman who was also a teacher, I made the adjustment and lived in San Diego from 1983 until 2001, spending about fifteen years back in a stateside setting, I made several returns to Europe.

Most often these rerturns were Christmas visits to Germany and visits to my daughter, Liane Stell and also to my ex-wife, Brigitte Stell whom I never ever really gave up as an integral part of my family.

She, after my four-year love affair with my beloved San Diego lady friend diminished, began to reunite with me as father of our beloved daughter, Liane Stell. After their adjustment to the divorce I deemed upon my ex-German wife in about 1986, our visits back and forth to Germany became more frequent as they even are today.

Returning to Germany, now in the vicinity of Bad Kreuznach, Germany, where I served as school administrator from 1977 to 1982, when

I left Germany permanently, became a permanent event for me. Returning during Christmas, to Germany, is a most lovable experience, especially the way the Germans celebrate this holiday.

But, not only Christmas, but other visits led me into other realms of Europe I had not experienced during my twenty-five exposure abroad! Having various love affairs in the United States often gave me travel partners back to Europe.

But the most productive affair I had while living back in the United States from 1983 until, even today, gave me the opportunity to either travel with a lady friend or alone and seek out areas I had not visited while living in Europe from 1961 until 1982.

One trip, other than the almost yearly Christmas visits proved to be quite illuminous. And this was a summer, about 1990, when I traveled to Splain with my Puerto Rican lady friend, who has a most distinguished family in San Diego. The young lady, was born in Puerto Rica and spoke English, Spanish, Portuguese, French, and was hitting my second language, German on our several visits back to Europe!

This lady, we will call her Anita, had a most prestigious family and her oldest sister was married to a wonderful person attached to a chain of McDonalds in and around San Diego.

Anita and I met in Madrid in the summer of about 1990 and traveled from Madrid down to southern Spain, then on to the coast of Portugal. We spent about ten days in Portugal, lounging in the beautiful sun, dancing Latin dances, and loving the area.

Anita, multi-lingual, was so hep in languages, it was a pleasure having her anywhere in Spain, France, and even Germany because she was a linguist! Her major at San Diego State University, where we both attended, I on sabbatical, and she as a regular student. Anita did not know mathematics but she could make set fire to any language related to the Romance languages!

What an inspiration. And being a native of Puerta Rico, she could make Latin dancing a thing of pure beauty.

We never considered marriage but being together for about four years made out lives in San Diego and Europe moments of envy! I brought he up to Hargesheim, Germany that summer and she chose to venture on to Switzerland and Austria, and Italy on her own. Sometimes it makes me rather sad to know I let her venture to those areas she had previously visited, alone. But it was her choice and our love was not deep enough to stay glued while enjoying the realms of Europe!

I also made several trips, alone, back to, first, Budapest, Hungary, exploring Buda and Pest, the lovely city giving me spicy food and Gypsy music which delighted the soul. This city had been described to me by a previous lady friend whom I met in New Orleans, while living in that fabulous city in 1958-59!

Liz Kulin was this lady's name and she bubbled when talking about beautiful Budapest. She got out of the area during the Hungarian Revolution when the Hungarians tried to break loose from the Russian domination behind the Iron Curtain, about 1956, which started in October and ended with the Russians putting a damper on it by November 4, 1956.

Liz Kulin, who ended up in the United States with various groups giving her aid to resettle in this country and she ended up in New Orleans where i met her. Liz, whom I dated for a couple of months, after meeting her on the St. Charlses streetcar which passed within about a hundred feet of my lovely St. Charles Ave. Apartment in the Garden District of New Orleans and only about ten blocks from her apartment, I knew nothing about Hungary and Liz gave me a book about Budapest which gave geographical and cultural information about this wonderful city.

Liz, at that time was in her late thirties and I was only about twenty-six years of age, proved to be too European for me, at that time, and very reserved, cautious about having me over to her apartment for overnight visits and too reserved to spend evenings with me, caused our relationship to soon diminish.

After returning to the United States, from my twenty-five years abroad, I returned to Germaany for one of my summer visits to Hargesheim, Germany, only a few kilometers from my past hometown of Bad Kreuznach and decided to take a trip from my ex-wife's house, Brigitte, to Budapest, where I spent about ten days.

Brigitte, with her, then fiance, a computer specialist in software and a Ph.D. in the field, from Poland were near the area of Budapest. We spoke via telephone but did not get together while I was in Budapest. I lavished the culture and food, spicy and to my taste, listened to Gypsy music in some of the wonderful restaurants. I also visited a restaurant, and famous, called the Gundel. And it was not far from where much of the revolution of 1956 took place.

I remember telling the manager I am an American from San Diego so I definitely got special treatment. Being alone the hostess, a lovely Hungarian lady gave me unsolicited attention. I also learned the owner, at that time was an American, I believe, owner of one of the cosmetic lines popular in the United States.

It was very satisfying for me to know the Hungarians on that vicinity spoke German, and readily, with me. The Hungarian language, from my internet visitations is a Uralic languages connected to the Finnish language. Hungarian is one of the twenty-four official languages of the European Union.

The citizens of Budapest and throughout the area I traveled by train, spoke German with me more so than English. Fortunately my readiness to speak German in the area gave me a comfort zone for shopping, dining, site-seeing, and general communications as I moved about Buda and also Pest.

Budapest is really composed of these two cities and I found them to be most beautiful in beauty and structure.

I ventured out into the beautiful Danube River while visiting Budapest and the architecture along that area is breathtaking. The whole area is really something to behold. And I owe it to a lovely lady who was cast out of the area due to the Hungarian Revolution of 1956, leaving her husband behind to continue to integrate with the existing Communistic regime. I often wonder if the two ever got back together. Her ties with her beautiful city of Budapest must have been most trying and her positive experiences with the then very socialistic and communistic Hungary did give her medical benefits she often cited to me, that she did not have in our country, the United States. I hope she made the adjustment because I did not see Liz after January 1959!

While teaching in San Diego, 1984 to about 2001, I earned in my last several years, over ninety-thousand dollars a year because on top of my seventy-thousand dollars per year as a classroom teacher, I was reaping the benefits of my overseas, Department of Defense Overseas Dependent Schools retirement, toward the last several years of high school teaching in San Diego.

One year, about 1992 I reaped even a greater windfall in income in having a lucky streak at Viejas Casino, about twenty miles east of San Diego, I-8. I drove one of our counselors out for a session of video poker, for me and the game of keno for him. Both games were recreational for both of us and we went out to this particular casino about once a week.

My friend, was playing a keno video game and hit about six-thousand dollars. Since I drove him out to play that evening, probably a Friday evening, he handed me two-hundred dollars as a gift for driving him out. He had to go home, so I drove him back, then returned to put his money to work. I hit a jackpot for about two-thousand and sixty-dollars. THIS was the beginning of a LUCKY STREAK, I have never since been able to duplicate.

I had a Philippino girlfriend at that time and she loved to gamble. For the next three weekends, we hit sums of money that were, sfter the first hit:

First weekend…video poker… I was dealt a Royal Flush for $7,300!

The next weekend-I hit $8,600 on a keno hit…

The streak went on until I topped out at, over a two month period, at $35,000.

That year, about 1992, I declared over $120,000 in federal taxes. That year I took two trips to Europe. One during the summer and then a return for Christmas to visit my daughter and my ex-wife. Times were good and I had a most lucky year playing my favorite games of video poker and keno.

My next trip, after the windfall in gambling, (about 1992-93) which I learned to do after my return to the United States in about 1984, with my past ladyfriend with whom I lived for four years but never married, was to Germany and then I made my visit to the Czech Republic and visited several cities, including Berlin, a city I had not visited since about 1963, shortly after my marriage to Brititte.

So the city I spent about a week in (1992 or 1993) was Prague, the Czech Republic. And then I visited other cities near Berlin, Germany about that time. The freedom and beauty of returning to the Eastern Bloc was most invigorating for me.

While living in Germany from 1961 until 1982, I could onlyh visit the west zone cities, not under the Communist Bloc! The Russians had their hands on so many countries during this time period and we, as American civilians and military were restricted from visits at this time period.

The time, after the fall of the Berlin Wall in 1989 was a joyful revelation for Americans abroad! I, as an American teacher, then had the privilege of going back and exploring areas that had been controlled by the Russians so

I was like a person who had been released to explore extensively, as long as my finances would allow! It was paradise!

So the time from the fall of the Berlin Wall until, even now, proved to be a full loving and free cavern of joyfChapul exposure to areas we had never been able to enjoy during the years of 1961, when I lived in beautiful Germany, until the time I left in 1963!

CHAPTER 18

Living Abroad for Americans Today

Why should youth or adventurous young soul today, 2016, seek employment abroad? If I were a college graduate with a meaningful degree, today, in the year 2016, and wanted to live abroad, especially in Europe and try to break into either a business field or work with the United States govrnment, I would cast aside any veils of restrictions, take a significant offer, either by government of big business and be on my way!

The revelations of living abroad exposure for a young person, married or single, open so many doors to world vision and exposure, I cannot emphasize enough, the vastness and richness of these experiences!

When I first set foot on the shores of Tripoli, Libya, (1960) a foreign land fo me, the doors of life and contact with other cultures released me from the womb of my previously coveted love of provincial security! This provincial security was only a veil of SECURITY! When I was released from this veil, I then began to expand my concept of international perception! Living among other cultures, being exposed to other languages and ways of perceiving life, made me another person.

My exposure of living abroad may not compare with other persons who have traversed the globe and gotten tastes of the orient, the middle east, and in depth European experiences, but my intense living among African,

German, Italian, and Dutch society overy a span of ttenty-five years, has proven to be a live of INTENSE positive multi-culture revelations!

I woulde not trade my experiences with anyone because of these intense exposures to another languaage and another culture. Having lived in Germany for eighteen uyears gave me the chance to cultivate and digest a second culture, almost to the extent of becoming fully integrated into this culture.

My feelings toward the German people was almost to the extent of becoming one of them! My heritage does involve some German background.

The name, Stell, from what I have heard from other German people, means, Fargestell, or a part of a wagon. So my being must have been genetically, embedded with some Gernman connection. I somehow felt, all the years I was intimately associated with the German people from 1961 until today, that my blood and genes are close to the Germans.

When I returned to the United States, on my sabbatical at San Diego State University, I suffered from, almost traumatic separation from my ADOPTED culture. Speaking German daily, shopping in the stores, enjoying social events were a part of my life… "Going Native" was often used by snobbish American educators if one got too chummy with the natives of the country we were living in. But doig this, chatting at restaurants, bars, outdoor coffee houses, were all part of the process of knowing a people and their way of life!

Having lunch, dinner, socials and fmily gatherings in Germany became a way of life, keeping my daily duties as a teacher or school administrator was like going from one box to another. But there was also the constant motivations of the military to respect the culture of target country!

Readjusting to American culture took a few years and even when I return to visit Germany I fall right into the mold; think in German, dream in German and have deep feelings for my ex-inlaws and friends in Germany!

The impressions and brand the Germans imparted on my soul will always go with me. I have been back in the United States since 1984 for full implantation

Bit the memories, constant awareness of Germans visiting the United States will always be in my soul. So many people I meet ask me, after long conversations discussing their visits to Germany, if I am German or is my family German.

The experiences were and still are positive and I love the country with its variety of topography, villages, lakes, and metropolitan areas are almost indellibly embedded into my soul and I have no regrets for it!

So when I am talking with young people with the proper educaion and background to prepare them for a possible position in Germany or another nation, I can only encourage them to go abroad and experience what I experienced over twenty-five years!

Though the times today (2016) may present hurdles and dangers we, as Americans living abroad from 1960 until 1983), the challenges of working abroad, even with existing dangers, will chance the perspecive of the employee or worker venturing out from his or her protective provincial environment at home! Go out and seek the world, dwell in it, savor its offers; other cultures, languages, and challenges, which I believe can only enhance a person's being because of this exposure to other ways of life, language, and culture! Go out and expanc yuour persona, your existence, and way of life. Go out and experience how other parts of the world live!

CHAPTER 19

My Personae After Many Years Abroad

I was born in Tinsman, Arkansas, in 1932. Today I believe the population may be far less than it was in that year. I revisited Arkansas and lived in my purchased townhouse, Hot Springs Village, about 1970. I kept the townhouse until about 2007 when I got rid of it. I lived there from 2001 until 2005, trying to return to my roots, relive the wonderful days of my high school and college, with fishing and duck hiunting being the prime targets…only the fishing part worked.

At any rate my persona, from the 1930s depression days on through the 1950s around Arkansas were great experiences for observing the world, with a few travels from the age ten, when I visited my oldest brother's house at his lovely home on Bell Meade Island, Miami, Florida, when he flew for Pan American Airways in 1942 or so. My brother was a world traveled pilot who even flew the Pan American Clipper before World War II. So my immediate exposure to worldly ways started at about ten years of age.

I learned, via my model brother and he was a Pensacola pilot of the U. S. Navy, imparting unbelievable experiences he had harvested from living and training pilots in Java, East Indies (now Indonesia), in about 1940 before the Japanese began to move into such areas, leading to World War II.

My oldest brother, though I had eight brothers and three sisters, was probably the most influential person in my life. We were very close.

He even met with me, my wife, daughter and his daughter in Madrid, Spain, in about 1972 and had me and my, now ex-wife, bring his daughter, who had flown into Frankfurt, Germany, in our 1967 300SE Mercedes, to visit with him and his second wife.

He would not set foot onto German because of his strongly built disgust of the German people he acquired from allied military involvement, flying the Hump…across Idia, ferrying B-25s for the U. S. Ferry Command, on loan from Pan American to the U. S. government.

At any rate, I later in life, even recently, discovered, through my youngest sister, he had a tremendous hate for anything German…country, people, even my ex-wife. Though I admired him like no one else because his living abroad experiences were impeccable. He had lived in Java, Rio de Janeiro, Miami, Florida, Arkansas, California, and Wahington State.

This man had it all and influenced me in seeking the ABROAD EXPERIENCE! It was in my soul, especially after having the bachelot's drgree from the University of Arkansas and the master's degree from Vanderbilt University, Nashville, Tennessee!.

Living abroad taught me, this small town Arkansas lad, though I completed high school in Little Rock, Arkansas, to expand my perspective, accept other ways of life, other languages, other cultures and respect the broadness of our world!

My character, since high school, has, no doubt increased ten times in the ability to understand people, look at the world as a place I am well adapted to in its several billion population setting, My ability to accept other cultures, become liberal in perception of minorities, and love people has certainly improved since my child rearing in the segrated South has become so improved and positive, I would say immensely compared to what it would have been had I have married that sweet fiance I contemplated marrying when I was graduating from my undrgraduate college at the University of Arkansas, Monticello, Arkansas in the year 1957, year of my father's dying!

I am no longer the provincial product of my Southern upbringing, though I had the privilege of teaching and living in beautiful and gorgeous New Orleans in 1958-59! This experience also brought my attention to the beginning of my cultural expansion, even though the setting was in the South!

Little Rock, Nashville, New Orleans, Los Angeles, Tripoli, Berlin, Paris, London, Hamburg, Rome, Madrid, have all been elements in my life that have rebuilt my existence and character as a person of the world!

So, my persona, after living so many years abroad, is integrated into a self perception of one who has grasped the multicultured world. I am aware of other cultures, other people, other languages, other ways of life This book is not meant for people who are not entranced by reading, or by people who have NO interest in such matters outside of their own worlds…leave them alone…let them enjoy the day by day living and interest ONLY IN day by day events of life. Anyone who wants to read my injections into an attempt of breaking into a literary world, may find some interest in the things I have written about.

My persona, as I see it, is that I have taken my life, from a small town lad in Arkansas, expanded the realms of living, not only in the United States but also in Africa and Europe and the great places in the United States. New Orleans included as one of the most fasciniating places in the Unites States! This city, attacked by me, in 1958-1959, proved to be an enclave of exuberenc while I was there. I would almost say, that living in Europe, over twenty years proved to be powerful, life improving, and most exciting! But, the one year in my life, I must say to all the wonderful people of New

Orleans was OVERWHELMING! For some reason, this enclave, in the great United States, has a CHARM and BEAUTY that, I must say, surpasses other cities in the United States. I have had the pleasure of visiting New York City...a vast empire of culture, exotic architecture, Broadway plays, interesting sites, and deep cultural charm, as does Sas Francisco! But the charm of New Orleans, with a deep integral cultural beauty, and I only know a minor portion of its depth, is by far the most charming city I have ever known!

I have visited Berlin, Hamburg, Munich, Paris, Rome, Prague, Budapest, Madrid, and many other cities of Europe, but found no other place in the world that TURNS ME ON, as does New Orleans! Maybe it was my ONE year living there in 1958-1959 that overwhelmed me with its culture and charm!

Some people say, "There are: New York City, San Francisco, and New Orleans!" And, " There is Cincinnati." The previously mentioned cities... and thee is Boston,,,,,,most charming, I must mention, have a charm of their own, but New Orleans, with the pleasure of my living there as previously mentioned, will turn anyone with a little flare for CULTURE, completely on. Whether it is the bombastic and dynamic charm of the French Quarters or the sensous arousement of the gorgeous uptown area where I lived, along St. Charles Avenue; "The Garden District," a paragon of beauty and charm, that can ONLY be aroused when one has the WONDERFUL PLEASURE AND FORTUNE OF ACTUALLY LIVING THERE! I do not believe the area of Central Park in New York or the, gorgeous near the bay areas and neighborhoods of San Francisco, have the charm of such a place as New Orlens.

My twenty-five years abroad were stimulating, but why would such a place as New Orleans remain in my memories for so long? Only one answer, this lovely city, in its historical setting, has remained a city of charm, of exquisite beauty, and has maintained a cultural enigma with a solid mixture of French Cajun inculcation, family trust and legal integrity espoused by no other city in the United States! These are just a few of my observations!

The school I taught in, Metairie, Lousiana, Ridgewood Preparatory School shall endure, from my one year experience, and remain a cultural POSITIVE in the realm of education for elementary and secondary students. It has flair educational greatness in the PRIVATE SCHOOL arena! I was overwhelmed by the eliteness and integral love the students gave.

I had the pleasure of being offered the school to purchase, about, 1970, by the previous owner, O. O. Stuckey, but could not muster the financies needed to purchase the school. What a flattering and gloriful compliment to me as an educator!

The school, which I visited…I would surmise, in about 1999 or so, had been purchased by someone, whom I met, and they had relocated! The owner was most humble and gracious because I was a teacher of 1958-59 vintage! I was treated with respect and honor because I was, not only a teacher under the original owner, O. O. Stuckey, but a friend who had been offered the school because of my auspicious trust in O. O. Stuckey!

This to me, is a mark of my career as an educator to be one of success!

I felt the past yars I had spent in education were SUCCESSFUL! Because of such fulfilling expeiences in this specific private school.

However, though monetarily well paid, the years of education on San Diego, though at the top of the teacher pay program, were a complete dsappointment because of my successful experience, as an educatior, in the Overseas Depandent School arena, from 19060 to 1982!.

My success and high attainments int OVERSEAS DEPENDENT SCHOOLS PROGRAM were superior to the levels I reached in the San Diego City Schools arena of education!

Returning to San Diego, to teach in about 1983, proved to be, in many ways, humiliating because I had attained a high levels of prestige with the Overseas Dependent Schools!.

My experiences with the San Diego San Diego Ciity Schools proved to be one of extreme disappointnent! My expertise in the administrative field did not mean anything to my evaluators in San Diego Unified School District, with ist overwhelming POLITICAL ARROGANCE!

I was a proven teacher to them and that is what they gave me credit for! Anytime I tried to break into the administrative field, they turned me down. Their own insecurity and distrust in themselves must have been their concept of me. I was, I felt at the TOP of my caliber and profile while in the Ovrseas Arena.

So my whole concept of trhe educational arena at San Diego was that of a successful administraor who could NEVER fit the profile of adaption in San Diego, California. Had I have been an integral part of their program from the beginning, i.e. while I lavished in the overseas arena from 1960 until 1982, my success would, no doubt, have been spectacular!

But the successes as a classroom teacher while teaching in San Diego from 1984 util 2001 only proved that I was a successful educator. The unyielding egotistical self engrossed insecure structure of the educational structure at San Diego City Schools while I was there proved to be one of a sad existence!

To blow my own horn, I can only reflect back on about 1975 or 1976, when I applied for a position as head administrator at one of nine elementary schools at Fort Benning, Georgia. I would have been one of nine administrators at one of these Department of Defense supported schools. In the elimination process where fifty Overseas Dependent School principals and vice-principals were selected, based on their application forms. I got word that twenty-five were eliminated. Remaining were twent-five of us, I included! Then I heard there were ten remaining and I, Larry B. Stell was still in the litter. Then there were five remaining; I was still in the pack. THEN there were two remaining! I was one of them!

Taking two days off for a nearby administrators' conference I got word that of the two, **I WAS** eliminated. The reason being that all my experience was in high school. I and my wife were anticipating a return to CONUS (Continental United States) so I could serve as one of the elementary principals at Fort Benning, Georgia.

This was one of the most disappointing experiences as an administrator! I and my principal decided I was eligible for a sabattical and this estitles one to half-pay while studying at any given university or college in the U.S.

I applied for the sabattical and was granted the leave with half-pay, so I chose San Diego State University, a place I served in the U. S. Navy for over a year. I knew the territory and had no problem setting up my course of study; part school administration and part German. I completed a major in German, studying at San Diego State and UCSD.

But this experience, though very successful, brought other events in my live and later led to the sad separation from my daughter and, now ex-wife!

When I did return to the Overseas Dependent Schools, I was placed in the elementary school in Kitzingen, Germany. I had been seeking such a school and had, of course, letit be known. The director of the Dependent Schools found a suitable position so I could gain the elementary administration experience. I accepted the position but only remained about three months in 1984.

I retired from the Overseas Dependent Schools in good standing but chose to give them up for a new experience in San Diego, along with a beautiful lady, her name I will not mention. She gave up her husband who was one of the upper echelon with San Diego Unified Schools!

So my point in this chapter, My Persona After Many Years Abroad, leadesme to summarize by stating my twenty-five years abroad was an integral part of learning to live in other cultures, learn another language and have the most beautiful countries of Europe as my home. Those three countries being Germany, Italy, and the Netherlands, in that order. My first year in Libya,North Africa was also an injection of a country where we then had a U. S. Air Base but later lost it to its past leader, Muammar Gaddafi, who died in October 2011.

When I lived there, the ruler's name was King Idris Senuss who lost power to Muammar Gaddafi in 1969. When I was in Tripoli, Libya, from September 1960 until late January 1961 but was transferred to Ramstein, Germany. My impressions of Libya at the time I was there in a desert land lying on the North coast of Africa, along the Mediterranean Sea, I found the setting interesting; desert, beautiful sea and mountains to the south. But the people were poor and often had their hands, especially to us (Americans).

But with Roman ruins to the east of the city and to the west, there were many interesting sites in this desert setting. I loved the Italian restaurants, with many remnants of the Italians who overruled the country prior to the King Idris regime.

So the experience for me, a young teacher for the Americans in a strange country; and I also substituted for the existing oil companies school, somewhat small but hosting oil company students; the whole Libyan experience is certainly not to be dismissed as a cultural loss. I tried the Arabic language with a few lessons, learned some expressions and phrases of a very difficult language, dedinitely foreign to my American English tongue!

All in all this was a very exotic experience. After I left, Gaffafi took control of the country in about 1969 but I was safe in the school where I taught in Brunssum, the Netherlands!

So my persona after many years abroad certainly was enhanced by multiple cultural and linguistic exposures, making me a person who certainly saw the European side of life from 1961 until about 1982! I would not trade these experiences for any better paying job teaching, which I could have had in California or even New York! I am credentialed in both states for secondary teaching, with administrative crentials allowing me to be an elementary or secondary administrator.

But now I am retired and love the Personae I acquired living abroad for the twenty-five years!

END

www.ingramcontent.com/pod-product-compliance
Lightning Source LLC
Chambersburg PA
CBHW030909080526
44589CB00010B/218